TEACHER'S PET PUBLICATIONS

PUZZLE PACK
for
The Red Badge of Courage

based on the book by
Stephen Crane

Written by
William T. Collins

© 2005 Teacher's Pet Publications
All Rights Reserved

The materials in this packet are copyrighted
by Teacher's Pet Publications, Inc.

These pages may be duplicated by the purchaser
for use in the purchaser's own classroom.

Copying any of these materials and distributing them
for any other purpose is a violation of the copyright laws.

© 2005 Teacher's Pet Publications, Inc.
www.tpet.com

INTRODUCTION
If you already own the LitPlan for this title, this Puzzle Pack will refresh your Unit Resource Materials and Vocabulary Resource Materials sections plus give you additional materials you can substitute into the tests. If you do not already have a complete LitPlan, these pages will give you some supplemental materials to use with your own plan. There are two main groups of materials: one set for unit words (such as characters' names, symbols, places, etc.) and one set for vocabulary words associated with the book.

WORD LIST
There is a word list for both the unit words and the vocabulary words. These lists show you which words are being used in the materials and the clues or definitions being used for those words. You may want to give students a word list with clues/definitions to help them, or you may want students to only have a word list (without clues/definitions) if you want them to work a little harder. Both are available for duplication. The word lists can also be your "calling key" for the bingo games.

FILL IN THE BLANK AND MATCHING
There are 4 each of the fill in the blank and matching worksheets for both the unit and vocabulary words. These pages can be used either as extra worksheets for students or as objective parts of a unit test. They can be done individually if students need extra help or as a whole class activity to review the material covered.

MAGIC SQUARES
The magic squares not only reinforce the material covered but also work on reasoning and math skills. Many teachers have told us that their students really enjoy doing these!

WORD SEARCH PUZZLES
The word search words go in all directions, as indicated on your answer keys. Two of the word search puzzles have the clues listed rather than the words. This makes the puzzle a little more difficult, but it reinforces the material better. Two word search puzzles have words only for students who find the clue puzzles too difficult.

CROSSWORD PUZZLES
Both unit and vocabulary word sections have 4 crossword puzzles.

BINGO CARDS
There are 32 individual bingo cards for the unit words and 32 individual bingo cards for the vocabulary words. You can use your word list as a "call list," calling the words at random and marking them off of your list as you go, or you could use the flash cards by cutting them apart and drawing the words at random from a hat (or box or whatever). To make a better review, you might ask for the definition and spelling of each word as you call it out–or you could call out the definitions and have students tell you the words they need to look for on the puzzle.

JUGGLE LETTERS
The vocabulary juggle letter game is intended to help students learn the spellings of the words. One sheet has the definitions listed on it as an extra help for students who need it or to reinforce the definitions if you choose to do so.

FLASH CARDS
We've included a set of vocabulary flash cards you can duplicate, cut, and fold for your students. Some teachers make a few sets for general use by the class; others make a set for each student. Some teachers duplicate them for each student and have the students cut & fold their own. You can cut out just the words and put them in a hat, have each student pick out one word and write the definition and a sentence for that word. Students then swap words and papers, with the next student adding a sentence of his own under the last one. You can have students swap as many times as you like. Each time the student will read the sentences written prior to his own and then add a sentence. You can cut out the words and definitions separately and play "I Have; Who Has?" Each student in the room draws a word and definition. The first student says, "I have (the name of the word). Who has the definition?" The student with the definition reads it then says, "I have (the name of the vocabulary word she has). Who has the definition?" The round continues until all words and definitions have been given.

Red Badge of Courage Word List

No.	Word	Clue/Definition
1.	ARTILLERY	The big guns; cannon, for example
2.	BADGE	Red ____ of Courage
3.	BATTLE	An episode of fighting
4.	BLOOD	Red fluid on soldiers' bandages
5.	CHAPEL	Place in forest where Henry came upon the dead soldier
6.	CONKLIN	Tall soldier Jim
7.	CORPSE	Dead body
8.	COURAGE	Bravery
9.	CRANE	Author Stephen
10.	DEAD	Henry wished he were ____, so he wouldn't have to face his embarrassing retreat.
11.	FEAR	Feeling of being afraid
12.	FLAG	Henry carried it into battle
13.	FOE	Enemy
14.	HENRY	Soldier Fleming
15.	HERO	One others exalt because of his deeds
16.	KILLED	Henry thought it would be better to get ____ directly.
17.	KNIGHT	He had slept and awakening had found himself a ____.
18.	LUNKHEADS	What the soldiers called their inept commanders
19.	MOTHER	Henry should not shirk his duty because of her.
20.	OFFICERS	They give commands.
21.	OMNISCIENT	Point of view from which the story is written
22.	ORDER	Command soldiers follow
23.	OUTCAST	Henry felt like a mental ____.
24.	PERSONIFICATION	Giving human characteristics to inhuman things
25.	PICTURESQUE	The officers neglected to stand in ____ attitudes.
26.	POWER	Henry endowed the flag with this because no harm could come to it.
27.	REALISTIC	Seeing things as they really are; not romantic
28.	REGIMENT	Military unit consisting of Battalion, et al.
29.	RETREAT	Go backward; lose ground in battle
30.	RIFLE	Long gun
31.	ROMANTIC	Unrealistic; seeing things rosier than they really are
32.	RUN	Henry's first concern was that he would ____ from battle.
33.	SHAME	The retreat of the mule drivers was a march of ____ to Henry.
34.	SHOT	Henry lies about his wound and says he was ____.
35.	SIN	Henry's ____ was deserting the tattered soldier.
36.	SMOKE	Firing gunpowder caused this, which made seeing difficult.
37.	SQUIRREL	Henry threw a pine cone at one, and it ran away.
38.	SYMBOL	Something that stands for something else
39.	TATTERED	Man Henry left in the man's time of need: ____ soldier
40.	THICKET	Dense growth of shrubs and underbrush
41.	WAR	The Civil ____
42.	WATER	Liquid in soldiers' canteens
43.	WILSON	The loud soldier
44.	WOUND	Injury; where a bullet may have hit, for example

Red Badge of Courage Fill In The Blanks 1

_____ 1. An episode of fighting
_____ 2. Henry should not shirk his duty because of her.
_____ 3. Unrealistic; seeing things rosier than they really are
_____ 4. Dense growth of shrubs and underbrush
_____ 5. Point of view from which the story is written
_____ 6. Red ____ of Courage
_____ 7. Man Henry left in the man's time of need: ____ soldier
_____ 8. Military unit consisting of Battalion, et al.
_____ 9. Giving human characteristics to inhuman things
_____ 10. Tall soldier Jim
_____ 11. Henry felt like a mental ____.
_____ 12. Injury; where a bullet may have hit, for example
_____ 13. Henry carried it into battle
_____ 14. Author Stephen
_____ 15. Henry threw a pine cone at one, and it ran away.
_____ 16. The big guns; cannon, for example
_____ 17. The loud soldier
_____ 18. The retreat of the mule drivers was a march of ____ to Henry.
_____ 19. Henry endowed the flag with this because no harm could come to it.
_____ 20. Go backward; lose ground in battle

Red Badge of Courage Fill In The Blanks 1 Answer Key

BATTLE	1. An episode of fighting
MOTHER	2. Henry should not shirk his duty because of her.
ROMANTIC	3. Unrealistic; seeing things rosier than they really are
THICKET	4. Dense growth of shrubs and underbrush
OMNISCIENT	5. Point of view from which the story is written
BADGE	6. Red ____ of Courage
TATTERED	7. Man Henry left in the man's time of need: ____ soldier
REGIMENT	8. Military unit consisting of Battalion, et al.
PERSONIFICATION	9. Giving human characteristics to inhuman things
CONKLIN	10. Tall soldier Jim
OUTCAST	11. Henry felt like a mental ____.
WOUND	12. Injury; where a bullet may have hit, for example
FLAG	13. Henry carried it into battle
CRANE	14. Author Stephen
SQUIRREL	15. Henry threw a pine cone at one, and it ran away.
ARTILLERY	16. The big guns; cannon, for example
WILSON	17. The loud soldier
SHAME	18. The retreat of the mule drivers was a march of ____ to Henry.
POWER	19. Henry endowed the flag with this because no harm could come to it.
RETREAT	20. Go backward; lose ground in battle

Red Badge of Courage Fill In The Blanks 2

_____ 1. Go backward; lose ground in battle

_____ 2. They give commands.

_____ 3. Feeling of being afraid

_____ 4. Military unit consisting of Battalion, et al.

_____ 5. Henry's ____ was deserting the tattered soldier.

_____ 6. Bravery

_____ 7. He had slept and awakening had found himself a ____.

_____ 8. Henry should not shirk his duty because of her.

_____ 9. Injury; where a bullet may have hit, for example

_____ 10. What the soldiers called their inept commanders

_____ 11. Place in forest where Henry came upon the dead soldier

_____ 12. The Civil ____

_____ 13. One others exalt because of his deeds

_____ 14. Giving human characteristics to inhuman things

_____ 15. Henry thought it would be better to get ____ directly.

_____ 16. The officers neglected to stand in ____ attitudes.

_____ 17. An episode of fighting

_____ 18. Henry lies about his wound and says he was _____.

_____ 19. The big guns; cannon, for example

_____ 20. Soldier Fleming

Red Badge of Courage Fill In The Blanks 2 Answer Key

RETREAT	1. Go backward; lose ground in battle
OFFICERS	2. They give commands.
FEAR	3. Feeling of being afraid
REGIMENT	4. Military unit consisting of Battalion, et al.
SIN	5. Henry's ____ was deserting the tattered soldier.
COURAGE	6. Bravery
KNIGHT	7. He had slept and awakening had found himself a ____.
MOTHER	8. Henry should not shirk his duty because of her.
WOUND	9. Injury; where a bullet may have hit, for example
LUNKHEADS	10. What the soldiers called their inept commanders
CHAPEL	11. Place in forest where Henry came upon the dead soldier
WAR	12. The Civil ____
HERO	13. One others exalt because of his deeds
PERSONIFICATION	14. Giving human characteristics to inhuman things
KILLED	15. Henry thought it would be better to get ____ directly.
PICTURESQUE	16. The officers neglected to stand in ____ attitudes.
BATTLE	17. An episode of fighting
SHOT	18. Henry lies about his wound and says he was ____.
ARTILLERY	19. The big guns; cannon, for example
HENRY	20. Soldier Fleming

Red Badge of Courage Fill In The Blanks 3

_____ 1. Point of view from which the story is written

_____ 2. One others exalt because of his deeds

_____ 3. The loud soldier

_____ 4. The Civil ____

_____ 5. The big guns; cannon, for example

_____ 6. Henry endowed the flag with this because no harm could come to it.

_____ 7. Henry carried it into battle

_____ 8. Bravery

_____ 9. Author Stephen

_____ 10. Liquid in soldiers' canteens

_____ 11. Place in forest where Henry came upon the dead soldier

_____ 12. What the soldiers called their inept commanders

_____ 13. Henry wished he were ____, so he wouldn't have to face his embarrassing retreat.

_____ 14. Dead body

_____ 15. Henry thought it would be better to get ____ directly.

_____ 16. Tall soldier Jim

_____ 17. An episode of fighting

_____ 18. Henry's ____ was deserting the tattered soldier.

_____ 19. Red fluid on soldiers' bandages

_____ 20. Seeing things as they really are; not romantic

Red Badge of Courage Fill In The Blanks 3 Answer Key

OMNISCIENT	1. Point of view from which the story is written
HERO	2. One others exalt because of his deeds
WILSON	3. The loud soldier
WAR	4. The Civil ____
ARTILLERY	5. The big guns; cannon, for example
POWER	6. Henry endowed the flag with this because no harm could come to it.
FLAG	7. Henry carried it into battle
COURAGE	8. Bravery
CRANE	9. Author Stephen
WATER	10. Liquid in soldiers' canteens
CHAPEL	11. Place in forest where Henry came upon the dead soldier
LUNKHEADS	12. What the soldiers called their inept commanders
DEAD	13. Henry wished he were ____, so he wouldn't have to face his embarrassing retreat.
CORPSE	14. Dead body
KILLED	15. Henry thought it would be better to get ____ directly.
CONKLIN	16. Tall soldier Jim
BATTLE	17. An episode of fighting
SIN	18. Henry's ____ was deserting the tattered soldier.
BLOOD	19. Red fluid on soldiers' bandages
REALISTIC	20. Seeing things as they really are; not romantic

Red Badge of Courage Fill In The Blanks 4

1. The retreat of the mule drivers was a march of ____ to Henry.
2. Henry threw a pine cone at one, and it ran away.
3. Go backward; lose ground in battle
4. The officers neglected to stand in ____ attitudes.
5. Injury; where a bullet may have hit, for example
6. He had slept and awakening had found himself a ____.
7. Point of view from which the story is written
8. Military unit consisting of Battalion, et al.
9. Tall soldier Jim
10. Giving human characteristics to inhuman things
11. One others exalt because of his deeds
12. The loud soldier
13. They give commands.
14. Henry's first concern was that he would ____ from battle.
15. The Civil ____
16. Unrealistic; seeing things rosier than they really are
17. Enemy
18. Red fluid on soldiers' bandages
19. Henry wished he were ____, so he wouldn't have to face his embarrassing retreat.
20. Henry endowed the flag with this because no harm could come to it.

Red Badge of Courage Fill In The Blanks 4 Answer Key

SHAME	1. The retreat of the mule drivers was a march of ____ to Henry.
SQUIRREL	2. Henry threw a pine cone at one, and it ran away.
RETREAT	3. Go backward; lose ground in battle
PICTURESQUE	4. The officers neglected to stand in ____ attitudes.
WOUND	5. Injury; where a bullet may have hit, for example
KNIGHT	6. He had slept and awakening had found himself a ____.
OMNISCIENT	7. Point of view from which the story is written
REGIMENT	8. Military unit consisting of Battalion, et al.
CONKLIN	9. Tall soldier Jim
PERSONIFICATION	10. Giving human characteristics to inhuman things
HERO	11. One others exalt because of his deeds
WILSON	12. The loud soldier
OFFICERS	13. They give commands.
RUN	14. Henry's first concern was that he would ____ from battle.
WAR	15. The Civil ____
ROMANTIC	16. Unrealistic; seeing things rosier than they really are
FOE	17. Enemy
BLOOD	18. Red fluid on soldiers' bandages
DEAD	19. Henry wished he were ____, so he wouldn't have to face his embarrassing retreat.
POWER	20. Henry endowed the flag with this because no harm could come to it.

Red Badge of Courage Matching 1

___ 1. SQUIRREL
___ 2. WILSON
___ 3. RIFLE
___ 4. PERSONIFICATION
___ 5. BADGE
___ 6. KNIGHT
___ 7. WOUND
___ 8. SHAME
___ 9. ROMANTIC
___ 10. CORPSE
___ 11. COURAGE
___ 12. BATTLE
___ 13. SHOT
___ 14. CONKLIN
___ 15. SYMBOL
___ 16. BLOOD
___ 17. TATTERED
___ 18. CRANE
___ 19. FLAG
___ 20. ORDER
___ 21. RETREAT
___ 22. OFFICERS
___ 23. THICKET
___ 24. REALISTIC
___ 25. LUNKHEADS

A. Henry lies about his wound and says he was _____.
B. Dense growth of shrubs and underbrush
C. Tall soldier Jim
D. Command soldiers follow
E. Dead body
F. Something that stands for something else
G. What the soldiers called their inept commanders
H. Injury; where a bullet may have hit, for example
I. Bravery
J. Author Stephen
K. Seeing things as they really are; not romantic
L. Giving human characteristics to inhuman things
M. Go backward; lose ground in battle
N. Long gun
O. Red fluid on soldiers' bandages
P. The retreat of the mule drivers was a march of ____ to Henry.
Q. Henry carried it into battle
R. Unrealistic; seeing things rosier than they really are
S. Red ____ of Courage
T. The loud soldier
U. They give commands.
V. An episode of fighting
W. Henry threw a pine cone at one, and it ran away.
X. Man Henry left in the man's time of need: ____ soldier
Y. He had slept and awakening had found himself a ____.

Red Badge of Courage Matching 1 Answer Key

W - 1. SQUIRREL	A. Henry lies about his wound and says he was _____.
T - 2. WILSON	B. Dense growth of shrubs and underbrush
N - 3. RIFLE	C. Tall soldier Jim
L - 4. PERSONIFICATION	D. Command soldiers follow
S - 5. BADGE	E. Dead body
Y - 6. KNIGHT	F. Something that stands for something else
H - 7. WOUND	G. What the soldiers called their inept commanders
P - 8. SHAME	H. Injury; where a bullet may have hit, for example
R - 9. ROMANTIC	I. Bravery
E - 10. CORPSE	J. Author Stephen
I - 11. COURAGE	K. Seeing things as they really are; not romantic
V - 12. BATTLE	L. Giving human characteristics to inhuman things
A - 13. SHOT	M. Go backward; lose ground in battle
C - 14. CONKLIN	N. Long gun
F - 15. SYMBOL	O. Red fluid on soldiers' bandages
O - 16. BLOOD	P. The retreat of the mule drivers was a march of ____ to Henry.
X - 17. TATTERED	Q. Henry carried it into battle
J - 18. CRANE	R. Unrealistic; seeing things rosier than they really are
Q - 19. FLAG	S. Red ____ of Courage
D - 20. ORDER	T. The loud soldier
M - 21. RETREAT	U. They give commands.
U - 22. OFFICERS	V. An episode of fighting
B - 23. THICKET	W. Henry threw a pine cone at one, and it ran away.
K - 24. REALISTIC	X. Man Henry left in the man's time of need: ____ soldier
G - 25. LUNKHEADS	Y. He had slept and awakening had found himself a ____.

Red Badge of Courage Matching 2

___ 1. SYMBOL
___ 2. SIN
___ 3. LUNKHEADS
___ 4. RIFLE
___ 5. THICKET
___ 6. HENRY
___ 7. OMNISCIENT
___ 8. FOE
___ 9. DEAD
___ 10. SHAME
___ 11. REALISTIC
___ 12. HERO
___ 13. BATTLE
___ 14. CHAPEL
___ 15. ORDER
___ 16. MOTHER
___ 17. POWER
___ 18. COURAGE
___ 19. ROMANTIC
___ 20. OFFICERS
___ 21. FEAR
___ 22. OUTCAST
___ 23. CRANE
___ 24. RUN
___ 25. WILSON

A. Unrealistic; seeing things rosier than they really are
B. One others exalt because of his deeds
C. What the soldiers called their inept commanders
D. Point of view from which the story is written
E. The loud soldier
F. Henry's ____ was deserting the tattered soldier.
G. Henry wished he were ____, so he wouldn't have to face his embarrassing retreat.
H. Feeling of being afraid
I. They give commands.
J. An episode of fighting
K. Dense growth of shrubs and underbrush
L. Author Stephen
M. Henry should not shirk his duty because of her.
N. The retreat of the mule drivers was a march of ____ to Henry.
O. Soldier Fleming
P. Seeing things as they really are; not romantic
Q. Something that stands for something else
R. Long gun
S. Place in forest where Henry came upon the dead soldier
T. Henry felt like a mental ____.
U. Command soldiers follow
V. Henry endowed the flag with this because no harm could come to it.
W. Enemy
X. Henry's first concern was that he would ____ from battle.
Y. Bravery

Red Badge of Courage Matching 2 Answer Key

Q - 1. SYMBOL
F - 2. SIN
C - 3. LUNKHEADS
R - 4. RIFLE
K - 5. THICKET
O - 6. HENRY
D - 7. OMNISCIENT
W - 8. FOE
G - 9. DEAD
N - 10. SHAME
P - 11. REALISTIC
B - 12. HERO
J - 13. BATTLE
S - 14. CHAPEL
U - 15. ORDER
M - 16. MOTHER
V - 17. POWER
Y - 18. COURAGE
A - 19. ROMANTIC
I - 20. OFFICERS
H - 21. FEAR
T - 22. OUTCAST
L - 23. CRANE
X - 24. RUN
E - 25. WILSON

A. Unrealistic; seeing things rosier than they really are
B. One others exalt because of his deeds
C. What the soldiers called their inept commanders
D. Point of view from which the story is written
E. The loud soldier
F. Henry's ____ was deserting the tattered soldier.
G. Henry wished he were ____, so he wouldn't have to face his embarrassing retreat.
H. Feeling of being afraid
I. They give commands.
J. An episode of fighting
K. Dense growth of shrubs and underbrush
L. Author Stephen
M. Henry should not shirk his duty because of her.
N. The retreat of the mule drivers was a march of ____ to Henry.
O. Soldier Fleming
P. Seeing things as they really are; not romantic
Q. Something that stands for something else
R. Long gun
S. Place in forest where Henry came upon the dead soldier
T. Henry felt like a mental ____.
U. Command soldiers follow
V. Henry endowed the flag with this because no harm could come to it.
W. Enemy
X. Henry's first concern was that he would ____ from battle.
Y. Bravery

Red Badge of Courage Matching 3

___ 1. TATTERED   A. Injury; where a bullet may have hit, for example
___ 2. WILSON   B. Dense growth of shrubs and underbrush
___ 3. REGIMENT   C. Unrealistic; seeing things rosier than they really are
___ 4. WATER   D. The Civil ____
___ 5. SMOKE   E. Red ____ of Courage
___ 6. BATTLE   F. An episode of fighting
___ 7. RETREAT   G. Place in forest where Henry came upon the dead soldier
___ 8. ORDER   H. Firing gunpowder caused this, which made seeing difficult.
___ 9. ROMANTIC   I. The loud soldier
___10. COURAGE   J. Bravery
___11. RIFLE   K. Henry endowed the flag with this because no harm could come to it.
___12. THICKET   L. Enemy
___13. LUNKHEADS   M. Man Henry left in the man's time of need: ____ soldier
___14. CHAPEL   N. Henry carried it into battle
___15. FLAG   O. Henry wished he were ____, so he wouldn't have to face his embarrassing retreat.
___16. DEAD   P. Go backward; lose ground in battle
___17. RUN   Q. One others exalt because of his deeds
___18. FOE   R. Henry should not shirk his duty because of her.
___19. MOTHER   S. He had slept and awakening had found himself a ____.
___20. HERO   T. What the soldiers called their inept commanders
___21. WAR   U. Military unit consisting of Battalion, et al.
___22. BADGE   V. Henry's first concern was that he would ____ from battle.
___23. KNIGHT   W. Long gun
___24. POWER   X. Command soldiers follow
___25. WOUND   Y. Liquid in soldiers' canteens

Red Badge of Courage Matching 3 Answer Key

M - 1. TATTERED	A. Injury; where a bullet may have hit, for example
I - 2. WILSON	B. Dense growth of shrubs and underbrush
U - 3. REGIMENT	C. Unrealistic; seeing things rosier than they really are
Y - 4. WATER	D. The Civil ____
H - 5. SMOKE	E. Red ____ of Courage
F - 6. BATTLE	F. An episode of fighting
P - 7. RETREAT	G. Place in forest where Henry came upon the dead soldier
X - 8. ORDER	H. Firing gunpowder caused this, which made seeing difficult.
C - 9. ROMANTIC	I. The loud soldier
J - 10. COURAGE	J. Bravery
W - 11. RIFLE	K. Henry endowed the flag with this because no harm could come to it.
B - 12. THICKET	L. Enemy
T - 13. LUNKHEADS	M. Man Henry left in the man's time of need: ____ soldier
G - 14. CHAPEL	N. Henry carried it into battle
N - 15. FLAG	O. Henry wished he were ____, so he wouldn't have to face his embarrassing retreat.
O - 16. DEAD	P. Go backward; lose ground in battle
V - 17. RUN	Q. One others exalt because of his deeds
L - 18. FOE	R. Henry should not shirk his duty because of her.
R - 19. MOTHER	S. He had slept and awakening had found himself a ____.
Q - 20. HERO	T. What the soldiers called their inept commanders
D - 21. WAR	U. Military unit consisting of Battalion, et al.
E - 22. BADGE	V. Henry's first concern was that he would ____ from battle.
S - 23. KNIGHT	W. Long gun
K - 24. POWER	X. Command soldiers follow
A - 25. WOUND	Y. Liquid in soldiers' canteens

Red Badge of Courage Matching 4

___ 1. FLAG
___ 2. OMNISCIENT
___ 3. WATER
___ 4. ROMANTIC
___ 5. KNIGHT
___ 6. SHAME
___ 7. SIN
___ 8. BLOOD
___ 9. HERO
___ 10. CHAPEL
___ 11. HENRY
___ 12. WILSON
___ 13. FOE
___ 14. REGIMENT
___ 15. POWER
___ 16. RETREAT
___ 17. REALISTIC
___ 18. KILLED
___ 19. TATTERED
___ 20. FEAR
___ 21. LUNKHEADS
___ 22. CRANE
___ 23. ORDER
___ 24. RUN
___ 25. SHOT

A. Henry endowed the flag with this because no harm could come to it.
B. Soldier Fleming
C. Henry carried it into battle
D. Author Stephen
E. Military unit consisting of Battalion, et al.
F. Man Henry left in the man's time of need: ____ soldier
G. Feeling of being afraid
H. Liquid in soldiers' canteens
I. Enemy
J. Red fluid on soldiers' bandages
K. The retreat of the mule drivers was a march of ____ to Henry.
L. Command soldiers follow
M. Go backward; lose ground in battle
N. Point of view from which the story is written
O. Henry's ____ was deserting the tattered soldier.
P. Henry's first concern was that he would ____ from battle.
Q. The loud soldier
R. Place in forest where Henry came upon the dead soldier
S. Unrealistic; seeing things rosier than they really are
T. One others exalt because of his deeds
U. He had slept and awakening had found himself a ____.
V. What the soldiers called their inept commanders
W. Henry thought it would be better to get ____ directly.
X. Seeing things as they really are; not romantic
Y. Henry lies about his wound and says he was ____.

Red Badge of Courage Matching 4 Answer Key

C - 1.	FLAG	A. Henry endowed the flag with this because no harm could come to it.
N - 2.	OMNISCIENT	B. Soldier Fleming
H - 3.	WATER	C. Henry carried it into battle
S - 4.	ROMANTIC	D. Author Stephen
U - 5.	KNIGHT	E. Military unit consisting of Battalion, et al.
K - 6.	SHAME	F. Man Henry left in the man's time of need: ____ soldier
O - 7.	SIN	G. Feeling of being afraid
J - 8.	BLOOD	H. Liquid in soldiers' canteens
T - 9.	HERO	I. Enemy
R - 10.	CHAPEL	J. Red fluid on soldiers' bandages
B - 11.	HENRY	K. The retreat of the mule drivers was a march of ____ to Henry.
Q - 12.	WILSON	L. Command soldiers follow
I - 13.	FOE	M. Go backward; lose ground in battle
E - 14.	REGIMENT	N. Point of view from which the story is written
A - 15.	POWER	O. Henry's ____ was deserting the tattered soldier.
M - 16.	RETREAT	P. Henry's first concern was that he would ____ from battle.
X - 17.	REALISTIC	Q. The loud soldier
W - 18.	KILLED	R. Place in forest where Henry came upon the dead soldier
F - 19.	TATTERED	S. Unrealistic; seeing things rosier than they really are
G - 20.	FEAR	T. One others exalt because of his deeds
V - 21.	LUNKHEADS	U. He had slept and awakening had found himself a ____.
D - 22.	CRANE	V. What the soldiers called their inept commanders
L - 23.	ORDER	W. Henry thought it would be better to get ____ directly.
P - 24.	RUN	X. Seeing things as they really are; not romantic
Y - 25.	SHOT	Y. Henry lies about his wound and says he was ____.

Copyrighted

Red Badge of Courage Magic Squares 1

Match the definition with the vocabulary word. Put your answers in the magic squares below. When your answers are correct, all columns and rows will add to the same number.

A. ARTILLERY
B. HERO
C. PERSONIFICATION
D. REALISTIC
E. SMOKE
F. FLAG
G. KNIGHT
H. POWER
I. BADGE
J. SHAME
K. HENRY
L. PICTURESQUE
M. CORPSE
N. RETREAT
O. WILSON
P. SYMBOL

1. Go backward; lose ground in battle
2. He had slept and awakening had found himself a ____.
3. The officers neglected to stand in ____ attitudes.
4. The big guns; cannon, for example
5. Soldier Fleming
6. One others exalt because of his deeds
7. Dead body
8. Henry endowed the flag with this because no harm could come to it.
9. Firing gunpowder caused this, which made seeing difficult.
10. Something that stands for something else
11. Giving human characteristics to inhuman things
12. The retreat of the mule drivers was a march of ____ to Henry.
13. Seeing things as they really are; not romantic
14. Red ____ of Courage
15. Henry carried it into battle
16. The loud soldier

A=	B=	C=	D=
E=	F=	G=	H=
I=	J=	K=	L=
M=	N=	O=	P=

Red Badge of Courage Magic Squares 1 Answer Key

Match the definition with the vocabulary word. Put your answers in the magic squares below. When your answers are correct, all columns and rows will add to the same number.

A. ARTILLERY
B. HERO
C. PERSONIFICATION
D. REALISTIC
E. SMOKE
F. FLAG
G. KNIGHT
H. POWER
I. BADGE
J. SHAME
K. HENRY
L. PICTURESQUE
M. CORPSE
N. RETREAT
O. WILSON
P. SYMBOL

1. Go backward; lose ground in battle
2. He had slept and awakening had found himself a ____.
3. The officers neglected to stand in ____ attitudes.
4. The big guns; cannon, for example
5. Soldier Fleming
6. One others exalt because of his deeds
7. Dead body
8. Henry endowed the flag with this because no harm could come to it.
9. Firing gunpowder caused this, which made seeing difficult.
10. Something that stands for something else
11. Giving human characteristics to inhuman things
12. The retreat of the mule drivers was a march of ____ to Henry.
13. Seeing things as they really are; not romantic
14. Red ____ of Courage
15. Henry carried it into battle
16. The loud soldier

A=4	B=6	C=11	D=13
E=9	F=15	G=2	H=8
I=14	J=12	K=5	L=3
M=7	N=1	O=16	P=10

Red Badge of Courage Magic Squares 2

Match the definition with the vocabulary word. Put your answers in the magic squares below. When your answers are correct, all columns and rows will add to the same number.

A. COURAGE
B. OMNISCIENT
C. HENRY
D. RETREAT
E. BLOOD
F. REALISTIC
G. LUNKHEADS
H. RIFLE
I. REGIMENT
J. FOE
K. SYMBOL
L. HERO
M. BATTLE
N. WATER
O. ORDER
P. CHAPEL

1. Bravery
2. Liquid in soldiers' canteens
3. Enemy
4. Red fluid on soldiers' bandages
5. What the soldiers called their inept commanders
6. One others exalt because of his deeds
7. Place in forest where Henry came upon the dead soldier
8. Soldier Fleming
9. Command soldiers follow
10. Go backward; lose ground in battle
11. Long gun
12. Something that stands for something else
13. Military unit consisting of Battalion, et al.
14. Seeing things as they really are; not romantic
15. Point of view from which the story is written
16. An episode of fighting

A=	B=	C=	D=
E=	F=	G=	H=
I=	J=	K=	L=
M=	N=	O=	P=

Red Badge of Courage Magic Squares 2 Answer Key

Match the definition with the vocabulary word. Put your answers in the magic squares below. When your answers are correct, all columns and rows will add to the same number.

A. COURAGE
B. OMNISCIENT
C. HENRY
D. RETREAT
E. BLOOD
F. REALISTIC
G. LUNKHEADS
H. RIFLE
I. REGIMENT
J. FOE
K. SYMBOL
L. HERO
M. BATTLE
N. WATER
O. ORDER
P. CHAPEL

1. Bravery
2. Liquid in soldiers' canteens
3. Enemy
4. Red fluid on soldiers' bandages
5. What the soldiers called their inept commanders
6. One others exalt because of his deeds
7. Place in forest where Henry came upon the dead soldier
8. Soldier Fleming
9. Command soldiers follow
10. Go backward; lose ground in battle
11. Long gun
12. Something that stands for something else
13. Military unit consisting of Battalion, et al.
14. Seeing things as they really are; not romantic
15. Point of view from which the story is written
16. An episode of fighting

A=1	B=15	C=8	D=10
E=4	F=14	G=5	H=11
I=13	J=3	K=12	L=6
M=16	N=2	O=9	P=7

Red Badge of Courage Magic Squares 3

Match the definition with the vocabulary word. Put your answers in the magic squares below. When your answers are correct, all columns and rows will add to the same number.

A. WAR
B. REGIMENT
C. CORPSE
D. SMOKE
E. CHAPEL
F. OFFICERS
G. FLAG
H. SYMBOL
I. DEAD
J. BATTLE
K. HENRY
L. BLOOD
M. CONKLIN
N. COURAGE
O. RUN
P. BADGE

1. Something that stands for something else
2. Tall soldier Jim
3. Military unit consisting of Battalion, et al.
4. Soldier Fleming
5. An episode of fighting
6. Dead body
7. Red ____ of Courage
8. Place in forest where Henry came upon the dead soldier
9. Henry's first concern was that he would ____ from battle.
10. They give commands.
11. Henry wished he were ____, so he wouldn't have to face his embarrassing retreat.
12. Firing gunpowder caused this, which made seeing difficult.
13. The Civil ____
14. Red fluid on soldiers' bandages
15. Henry carried it into battle
16. Bravery

A=	B=	C=	D=
E=	F=	G=	H=
I=	J=	K=	L=
M=	N=	O=	P=

25
Copyrighted

Red Badge of Courage Magic Squares 3 Answer Key

Match the definition with the vocabulary word. Put your answers in the magic squares below. When your answers are correct, all columns and rows will add to the same number.

A. WAR
B. REGIMENT
C. CORPSE
D. SMOKE
E. CHAPEL
F. OFFICERS
G. FLAG
H. SYMBOL
I. DEAD
J. BATTLE
K. HENRY
L. BLOOD
M. CONKLIN
N. COURAGE
O. RUN
P. BADGE

1. Something that stands for something else
2. Tall soldier Jim
3. Military unit consisting of Battalion, et al.
4. Soldier Fleming
5. An episode of fighting
6. Dead body
7. Red ____ of Courage
8. Place in forest where Henry came upon the dead soldier
9. Henry's first concern was that he would ____ from battle.
10. They give commands.
11. Henry wished he were ____, so he wouldn't have to face his embarrassing retreat.
12. Firing gunpowder caused this, which made seeing difficult.
13. The Civil ____
14. Red fluid on soldiers' bandages
15. Henry carried it into battle
16. Bravery

A=13	B=3	C=6	D=12
E=8	F=10	G=15	H=1
I=11	J=5	K=4	L=14
M=2	N=16	O=9	P=7

Red Badge of Courage Magic Squares 4

Match the definition with the vocabulary word. Put your answers in the magic squares below. When your answers are correct, all columns and rows will add to the same number.

A. SIN
B. KILLED
C. BATTLE
D. SHOT
E. LUNKHEADS
F. RUN
G. CRANE
H. ORDER
I. OFFICERS
J. FOE
K. HENRY
L. RETREAT
M. SMOKE
N. TATTERED
O. ROMANTIC
P. SHAME

1. An episode of fighting
2. Enemy
3. Henry's first concern was that he would ____ from battle.
4. Unrealistic; seeing things rosier than they really are
5. The retreat of the mule drivers was a march of ____ to Henry.
6. What the soldiers called their inept commanders
7. They give commands.
8. Henry lies about his wound and says he was ____.
9. Firing gunpowder caused this, which made seeing difficult.
10. Command soldiers follow
11. Go backward; lose ground in battle
12. Henry's ____ was deserting the tattered soldier.
13. Henry thought it would be better to get ____ directly.
14. Soldier Fleming
15. Author Stephen
16. Man Henry left in the man's time of need: ____ soldier

A=	B=	C=	D=
E=	F=	G=	H=
I=	J=	K=	L=
M=	N=	O=	P=

Red Badge of Courage Magic Squares 4 Answer Key

Match the definition with the vocabulary word. Put your answers in the magic squares below. When your answers are correct, all columns and rows will add to the same number.

A. SIN
B. KILLED
C. BATTLE
D. SHOT
E. LUNKHEADS
F. RUN
G. CRANE
H. ORDER
I. OFFICERS
J. FOE
K. HENRY
L. RETREAT
M. SMOKE
N. TATTERED
O. ROMANTIC
P. SHAME

1. An episode of fighting
2. Enemy
3. Henry's first concern was that he would ____ from battle.
4. Unrealistic; seeing things rosier than they really are
5. The retreat of the mule drivers was a march of ____ to Henry.
6. What the soldiers called their inept commanders
7. They give commands.
8. Henry lies about his wound and says he was _____.
9. Firing gunpowder caused this, which made seeing difficult.
10. Command soldiers follow
11. Go backward; lose ground in battle
12. Henry's ____ was deserting the tattered soldier.
13. Henry thought it would be better to get ____ directly.
14. Soldier Fleming
15. Author Stephen
16. Man Henry left in the man's time of need: ____ soldier

A=12	B=13	C=1	D=8
E=6	F=3	G=15	H=10
I=7	J=2	K=14	L=11
M=9	N=16	O=4	P=5

Red Badge of Courage Word Search 1

Words are placed backwards, forward, diagonally, up and down. Clues listed below can help you find the words. Circle the hidden vocabulary words in the maze.

M	O	T	H	E	R	C	H	A	P	E	L	G	L	R	S	P	C
P	W	D	V	Q	G	R	C	O	U	R	A	G	E	Z	O	R	W
Z	P	A	Z	J	F	O	P	O	U	T	C	A	S	T	F	E	C
P	N	K	T	F	D	M	C	O	N	K	L	I	N	M	F	G	S
V	O	H	D	E	L	A	S	Q	U	I	R	R	E	L	I	I	X
N	M	W	A	D	R	N	Q	J	S	T	Y	E	D	E	C	M	Q
S	C	D	E	P	N	T	D	T	H	C	L	O	A	N	E	E	B
Y	K	F	X	R	I	I	I	E	O	T	O	R	R	A	R	N	B
M	Z	M	T	H	I	C	K	E	T	L	Y	E	T	R	S	T	N
B	G	N	L	W	N	O	T	A	B	R	F	H	I	C	H	A	N
O	O	U	C	O	M	R	B	U	N	K	G	F	L	E	A	T	G
L	C	R	S	S	Z	P	E	E	R	I	L	F	L	G	M	T	B
V	L	L	D	H	S	S	H	T	N	E	O	V	E	D	E	E	S
Y	I	X	W	E	S	E	F	K	R	E	S	D	R	A	C	R	X
W	X	S	Z	L	R	R	L	D	W	E	S	Q	Y	B	R	E	P
K	I	L	L	E	D	K	A	D	X	A	A	I	U	M	D	D	P
W	O	U	N	D	D	N	D	G	G	B	R	R	T	N	E	C	X

An episode of fighting (6)
Author Stephen (5)
Bravery (7)
Command soldiers follow (5)
Dead body (6)
Dense growth of shrubs and underbrush (7)
Enemy (3)
Feeling of being afraid (4)
Firing gunpowder caused this, which made seeing difficult. (5)
Go backward; lose ground in battle (7)
He had slept and awakening had found himself a ____. (6)
Henry carried it into battle (4)
Henry endowed the flag with this because no harm could come to it. (5)
Henry felt like a mental ____. (7)
Henry lies about his wound and says he was _____. (4)
Henry should not shirk his duty because of her. (6)
Henry thought it would be better to get ____ directly. (6)
Henry threw a pine cone at one, and it ran away. (8)
Henry wished he were ____, so he wouldn't have to face his embarrassing retreat. (4)
Henry's ____ was deserting the tattered soldier. (3)

Henry's first concern was that he would ____ from battle. (3)
Injury; where a bullet may have hit, for example (5)
Liquid in soldiers' canteens (5)
Long gun (5)
Man Henry left in the man's time of need: ____ soldier (8)
Military unit consisting of Battalion, et al. (8)
One others exalt because of his deeds (4)
Place in forest where Henry came upon the dead soldier (6)
Red ____ of Courage (5)
Red fluid on soldiers' bandages (5)
Seeing things as they really are; not romantic (9)
Soldier Fleming (5)
Something that stands for something else (6)
Tall soldier Jim (7)
The Civil ____ (3)
The big guns; cannon, for example (9)
The loud soldier (6)
The officers neglected to stand in ____ attitudes. (11)
The retreat of the mule drivers was a march of ____ to Henry. (5)
They give commands. (8)
Unrealistic; seeing things rosier than they really are (8)

Red Badge of Courage Word Search 1 Answer Key

Words are placed backwards, forward, diagonally, up and down. Clues listed below can help you find the words. Circle the hidden vocabulary words in the maze.

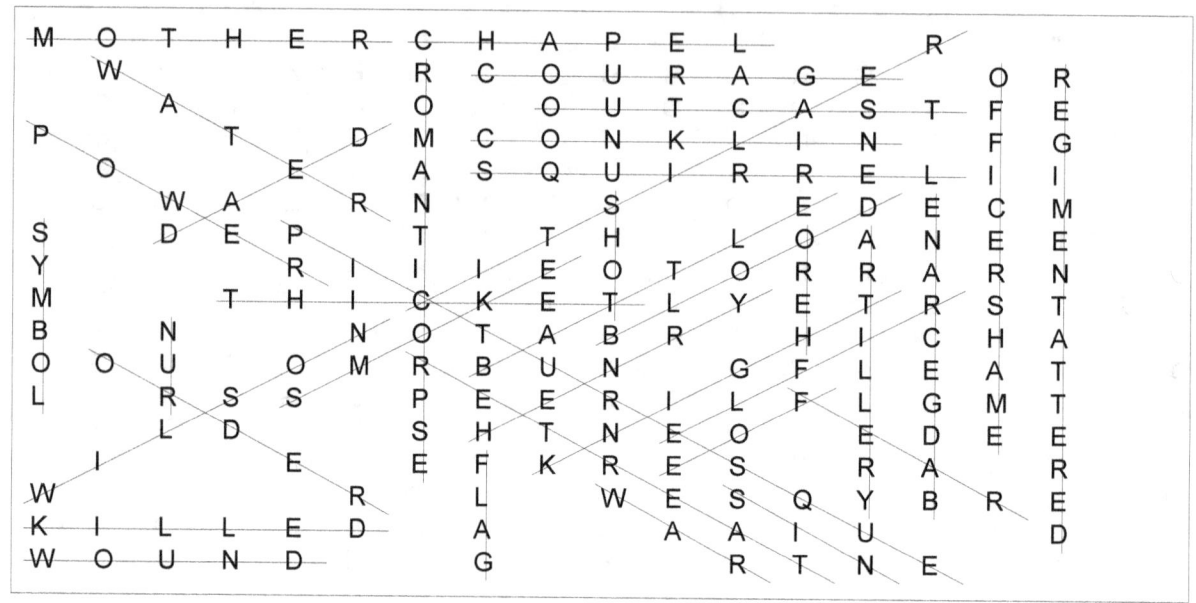

An episode of fighting (6)
Author Stephen (5)
Bravery (7)
Command soldiers follow (5)
Dead body (6)
Dense growth of shrubs and underbrush (7)
Enemy (3)
Feeling of being afraid (4)
Firing gunpowder caused this, which made seeing difficult. (5)
Go backward; lose ground in battle (7)
He had slept and awakening had found himself a ____. (6)
Henry carried it into battle (4)
Henry endowed the flag with this because no harm could come to it. (5)
Henry felt like a mental ____. (7)
Henry lies about his wound and says he was ____. (4)
Henry should not shirk his duty because of her. (6)
Henry thought it would be better to get ____ directly. (6)
Henry threw a pine cone at one, and it ran away. (8)
Henry wished he were ____, so he wouldn't have to face his embarrassing retreat. (4)
Henry's ____ was deserting the tattered soldier. (3)

Henry's first concern was that he would ____ from battle. (3)
Injury; where a bullet may have hit, for example (5)
Liquid in soldiers' canteens (5)
Long gun (5)
Man Henry left in the man's time of need: ____ soldier (8)
Military unit consisting of Battalion, et al. (8)
One others exalt because of his deeds (4)
Place in forest where Henry came upon the dead soldier (6)
Red ____ of Courage (5)
Red fluid on soldiers' bandages (5)
Seeing things as they really are; not romantic (9)
Soldier Fleming (5)
Something that stands for something else (6)
Tall soldier Jim (7)
The Civil ____ (3)
The big guns; cannon, for example (9)
The loud soldier (6)
The officers neglected to stand in ____ attitudes. (11)
The retreat of the mule drivers was a march of ____ to Henry. (5)
They give commands. (8)
Unrealistic; seeing things rosier than they really are (8)

Red Badge of Courage Word Search 2

Words are placed backwards, forward, diagonally, up and down. Clues listed below can help you find the words. Circle the hidden vocabulary words in the maze.

H	E	R	O	M	A	N	T	I	C	N	C	H	N	S	D	S	H
M	E	H	R	W	A	K	V	Z	X	O	H	D	E	H	D	K	
Q	A	G	M	S	E	A	G	I	Z	N	R	H	A	Z	S	O	C
M	H	I	S	R	P	W	T	R	L	P	P	D	T	P	J	R	T
R	S	M	T	E	M	K	J	E	F	L	S	Y	C	N	E	K	B
R	N	E	F	C	Z	Z	D	H	R	J	E	G	R	W	C	L	A
W	R	N	V	I	T	A	T	T	E	R	E	D	H	I	M	R	T
F	O	T	B	F	N	C	C	O	W	G	M	F	M	Q	F	S	T
F	W	U	V	F	L	O	B	M	Y	S	N	Z	Z	Q	G	L	L
V	P	I	N	O	Z	N	J	L	K	G	C	O	U	R	A	G	E
K	X	B	L	D	B	K	L	E	T	N	I	O	K	X	M	T	D
Q	N	Z	L	S	V	L	J	R	H	Z	T	L	R	P	H	F	J
W	M	I	T	M	O	I	G	R	I	M	S	W	C	D	Y	D	C
B	A	D	G	E	T	N	E	I	C	S	I	N	M	O	E	Y	Q
J	L	A	G	H	I	F	S	U	K	R	L	Q	W	S	K	R	Q
R	L	O	D	S	T	X	J	Q	E	F	A	S	A	Q	O	N	W
F	U	B	O	U	T	C	A	S	T	O	E	N	R	L	M	E	Z
W	G	N	B	D	P	O	W	E	R	E	A	E	F	S	H	B

An episode of fighting (6)
Author Stephen (5)
Bravery (7)
Command soldiers follow (5)
Dead body (6)
Dense growth of shrubs and underbrush (7)
Enemy (3)
Feeling of being afraid (4)
Firing gunpowder caused this, which made seeing difficult. (5)
Go backward; lose ground in battle (7)
He had slept and awakening had found himself a ____. (6)
Henry carried it into battle (4)
Henry endowed the flag with this because no harm could come to it. (5)
Henry felt like a mental ____. (7)
Henry lies about his wound and says he was ____. (4)
Henry should not shirk his duty because of her. (6)
Henry thought it would be better to get ____ directly. (6)
Henry threw a pine cone at one, and it ran away. (8)
Henry wished he were ____, so he wouldn't have to face his embarrassing retreat. (4)
Henry's ____ was deserting the tattered soldier.

____ (3)
Henry's first concern was that he would ____ from battle. (3)
Injury; where a bullet may have hit, for example (5)
Liquid in soldiers' canteens (5)
Long gun (5)
Man Henry left in the man's time of need: ____ soldier (8)
Military unit consisting of Battalion, et al. (8)
One others exalt because of his deeds (4)
Place in forest where Henry came upon the dead soldier (6)
Point of view from which the story is written (10)
Red ____ of Courage (5)
Red fluid on soldiers' bandages (5)
Seeing things as they really are; not romantic (9)
Soldier Fleming (5)
Something that stands for something else (6)
Tall soldier Jim (7)
The Civil ____ (3)
The loud soldier (6)
The retreat of the mule drivers was a march of ____ to Henry. (5)
They give commands. (8)
Unrealistic; seeing things rosier than they really are (8)

Red Badge of Courage Word Search 2 Answer Key

Words are placed backwards, forward, diagonally, up and down. Clues listed below can help you find the words. Circle the hidden vocabulary words in the maze.

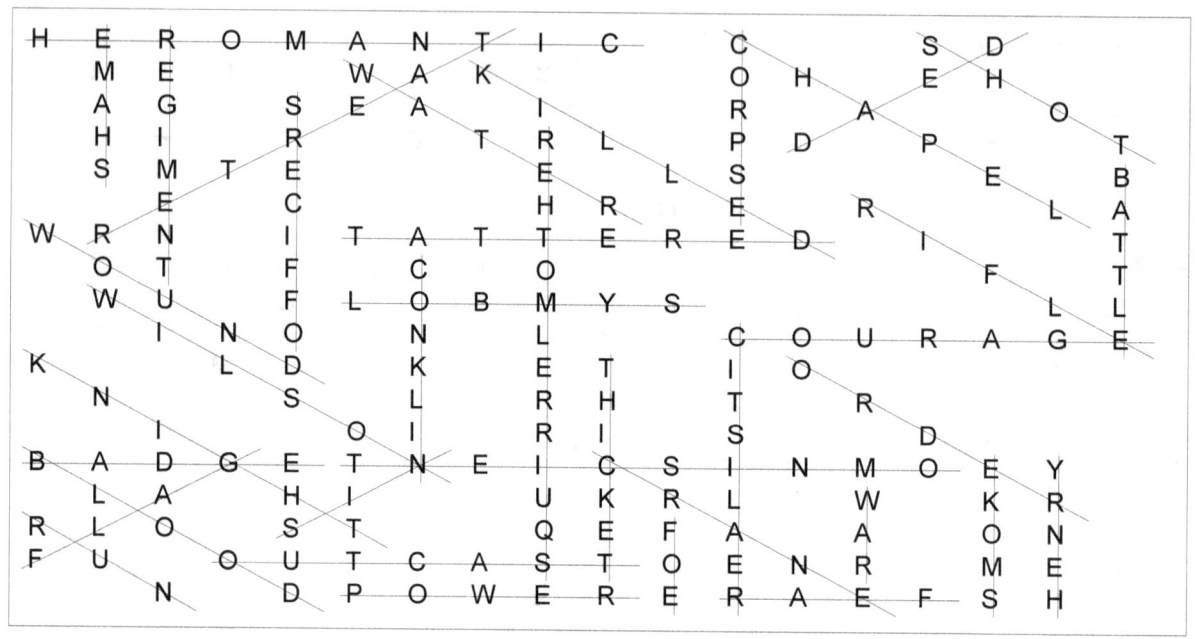

An episode of fighting (6)
Author Stephen (5)
Bravery (7)
Command soldiers follow (5)
Dead body (6)
Dense growth of shrubs and underbrush (7)
Enemy (3)
Feeling of being afraid (4)
Firing gunpowder caused this, which made seeing difficult. (5)
Go backward; lose ground in battle (7)
He had slept and awakening had found himself a _____. (6)
Henry carried it into battle (4)
Henry endowed the flag with this because no harm could come to it. (5)
Henry felt like a mental _____. (7)
Henry lies about his wound and says he was _____. (4)
Henry should not shirk his duty because of her. (6)
Henry thought it would be better to get _____ directly. (6)
Henry threw a pine cone at one, and it ran away. (8)
Henry wished he were _____, so he wouldn't have to face his embarrassing retreat. (4)
Henry's _____ was deserting the tattered soldier. (3)
Henry's first concern was that he would _____ from battle. (3)
Injury; where a bullet may have hit, for example (5)
Liquid in soldiers' canteens (5)
Long gun (5)
Man Henry left in the man's time of need: _____ soldier (8)
Military unit consisting of Battalion, et al. (8)
One others exalt because of his deeds (4)
Place in forest where Henry came upon the dead soldier (6)
Point of view from which the story is written (10)
Red _____ of Courage (5)
Red fluid on soldiers' bandages (5)
Seeing things as they really are; not romantic (9)
Soldier Fleming (5)
Something that stands for something else (6)
Tall soldier Jim (7)
The Civil _____ (3)
The loud soldier (6)
The retreat of the mule drivers was a march of _____ to Henry. (5)
They give commands. (8)
Unrealistic; seeing things rosier than they really are (8)

Red Badge of Courage Word Search 3

Words are placed backwards, forward, diagonally, up and down. Words listed below are included in the maze. Circle the hidden vocabulary words in the maze.

H	E	N	R	Y	C	O	N	K	L	I	N	M	G	P	O	W	E	R	B
K	N	P	I	C	T	U	R	E	S	Q	U	E	S	P	M	T	S	O	F
W	O	A	R	T	I	L	L	E	R	Y	G	S	V	T	N	B	Q	M	Y
C	I	T	S	I	L	A	E	R	H	A	N	L	S	T	I	F	U	A	K
R	T	M	F	J	Z	F	J	X	R	K	F	R	R	S	Y	I	N	Z
W	A	W	R	V	R	K	Z	U	T	C	C	E	T	T	C	R	R	T	V
C	C	I	M	C	Y	H	O	H	T	P	H	G	R	F	I	E	R	I	G
Z	I	L	R	W	O	C	H	B	H	T	V	I	W	Q	E	T	E	C	S
J	F	S	L	Z	R	R	V	S	I	W	Y	M	B	T	N	R	L	F	Z
R	I	O	C	Y	D	D	P	P	C	M	Z	E	L	A	T	E	N	T	H
J	N	N	K	P	E	J	K	S	K	P	O	N	C	K	T	A	A	W	T
F	O	F	E	A	R	I	F	L	E	O	U	T	C	A	S	T	F	A	B
C	S	S	G	U	L	H	U	G	T	P	O	L	H	R	T	H	L	R	J
F	R	S	N	L	N	N	D	P	T	H	E	Q	E	E	E	G	O	E	P
G	E	A	E	D	K	A	P	T	S	P	N	C	R	R	R	I	B	M	B
V	P	D	N	H	B	B	D	E	A	D	I	E	O	F	P	N	M	A	Z
D	F	U	E	E	B	L	F	H	M	F	D	K	Y	J	I	K	Y	H	R
R	O	A	F	G	B	O	C	L	F	Y	F	O	Q	S	P	M	S	S	B
W	D	S	C	M	W	O	S	O	A	Q	H	M	V	D	Z	R	J	S	W
S	J	N	X	R	G	D	W	K	B	G	X	S	W	A	T	E	R	T	L

ARTILLERY	FLAG	OUTCAST	SHOT
BADGE	FOE	PERSONIFICATION	SIN
BATTLE	HENRY	PICTURESQUE	SMOKE
BLOOD	HERO	POWER	SQUIRREL
CHAPEL	KILLED	REALISTIC	SYMBOL
CONKLIN	KNIGHT	REGIMENT	TATTERED
CORPSE	LUNKHEADS	RETREAT	THICKET
COURAGE	MOTHER	RIFLE	WAR
CRANE	OFFICERS	ROMANTIC	WATER
DEAD	OMNISCIENT	RUN	WILSON
FEAR	ORDER	SHAME	WOUND

Red Badge of Courage Word Search 3 Answer Key

Words are placed backwards, forward, diagonally, up and down. Words listed below are included in the maze. Circle the hidden vocabulary words in the maze.

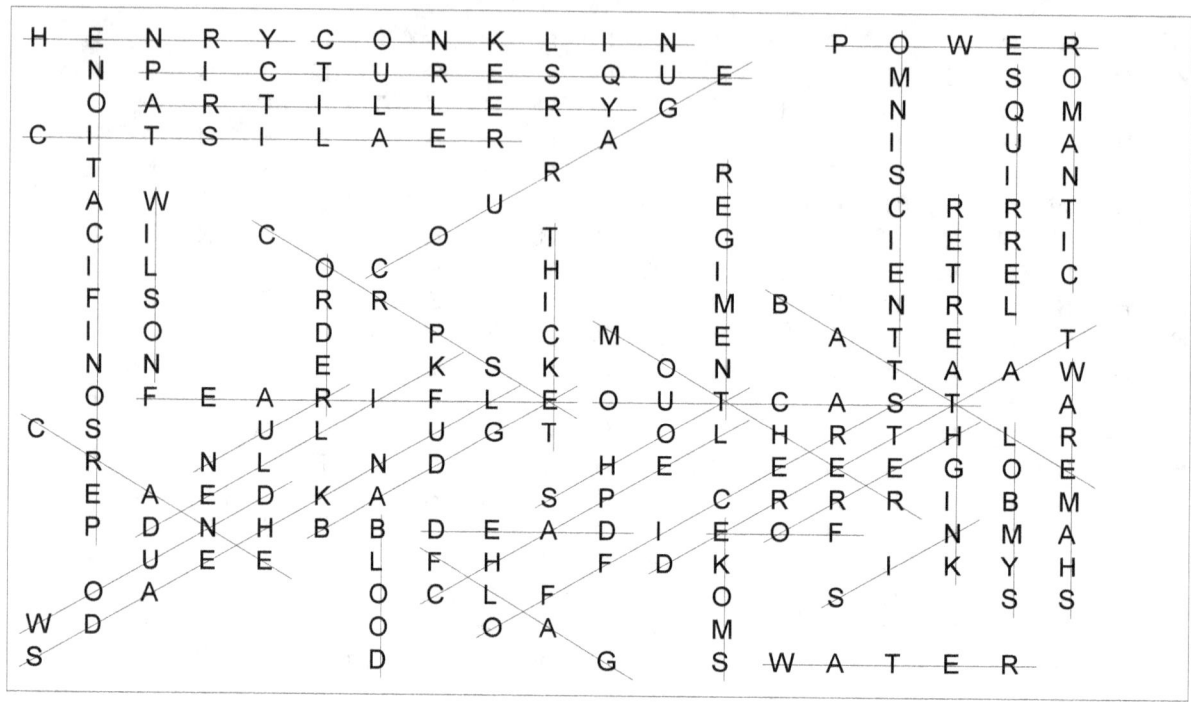

ARTILLERY	FLAG	OUTCAST	SHOT
BADGE	FOE	PERSONIFICATION	SIN
BATTLE	HENRY	PICTURESQUE	SMOKE
BLOOD	HERO	POWER	SQUIRREL
CHAPEL	KILLED	REALISTIC	SYMBOL
CONKLIN	KNIGHT	REGIMENT	TATTERED
CORPSE	LUNKHEADS	RETREAT	THICKET
COURAGE	MOTHER	RIFLE	WAR
CRANE	OFFICERS	ROMANTIC	WATER
DEAD	OMNISCIENT	RUN	WILSON
FEAR	ORDER	SHAME	WOUND

Red Badge of Courage Word Search 4

Words are placed backwards, forward, diagonally, up and down. Words listed below are included in the maze. Circle the hidden vocabulary words in the maze.

```
P E R S O N I F I C A T I O N S N V O M
S S V E H V P K P P L W L F V D Y Y U Z
S J F G T C T B S C D I V H F A T V T N
H Y X A H T L L J S T L C T V E D S C P
A E G R I V H O L H N S S R X H O H A P
M M R U C Z L O S H E O F B A K R O S M
E S M O K E G D A B I N W O U N D T T M
X D F C E G E G P Z C R R T E U E B M X
W E O G T R S A H Y S O Y Y J L R V F Y
L A F F E H S L L I M R K D N P C C Y
N D R T F R I F L E N A R E G I M E N T
K D T Z E I N C E P M N R L T R Z U M F
S A K W A V C L S A O T M T E R R L G R
T Y O K R M T E P H K I G T I J E N J Z
B P M R W H K R R C I C A A S L I A X W
J X F B G R G R O S L W H B M L L K T T
L J Y I O T R I C H L F C J K H G E D D
J Z N K Q L J U G L E R N N S K Q N R R
C K V L Y D B Q M J D G O D K B Q Q Q Y
M O T H E R G S Q L S C I T S I L A E R
```

ARTILLERY	FLAG	OUTCAST	SIN
BADGE	FOE	PERSONIFICATION	SMOKE
BATTLE	HENRY	POWER	SQUIRREL
BLOOD	HERO	REALISTIC	SYMBOL
CHAPEL	KILLED	REGIMENT	TATTERED
CONKLIN	KNIGHT	RETREAT	THICKET
CORPSE	LUNKHEADS	RIFLE	WAR
COURAGE	MOTHER	ROMANTIC	WATER
CRANE	OFFICERS	RUN	WILSON
DEAD	OMNISCIENT	SHAME	WOUND
FEAR	ORDER	SHOT	

Red Badge of Courage Word Search 4 Answer Key

Words are placed backwards, forward, diagonally, up and down. Words listed below are included in the maze. Circle the hidden vocabulary words in the maze.

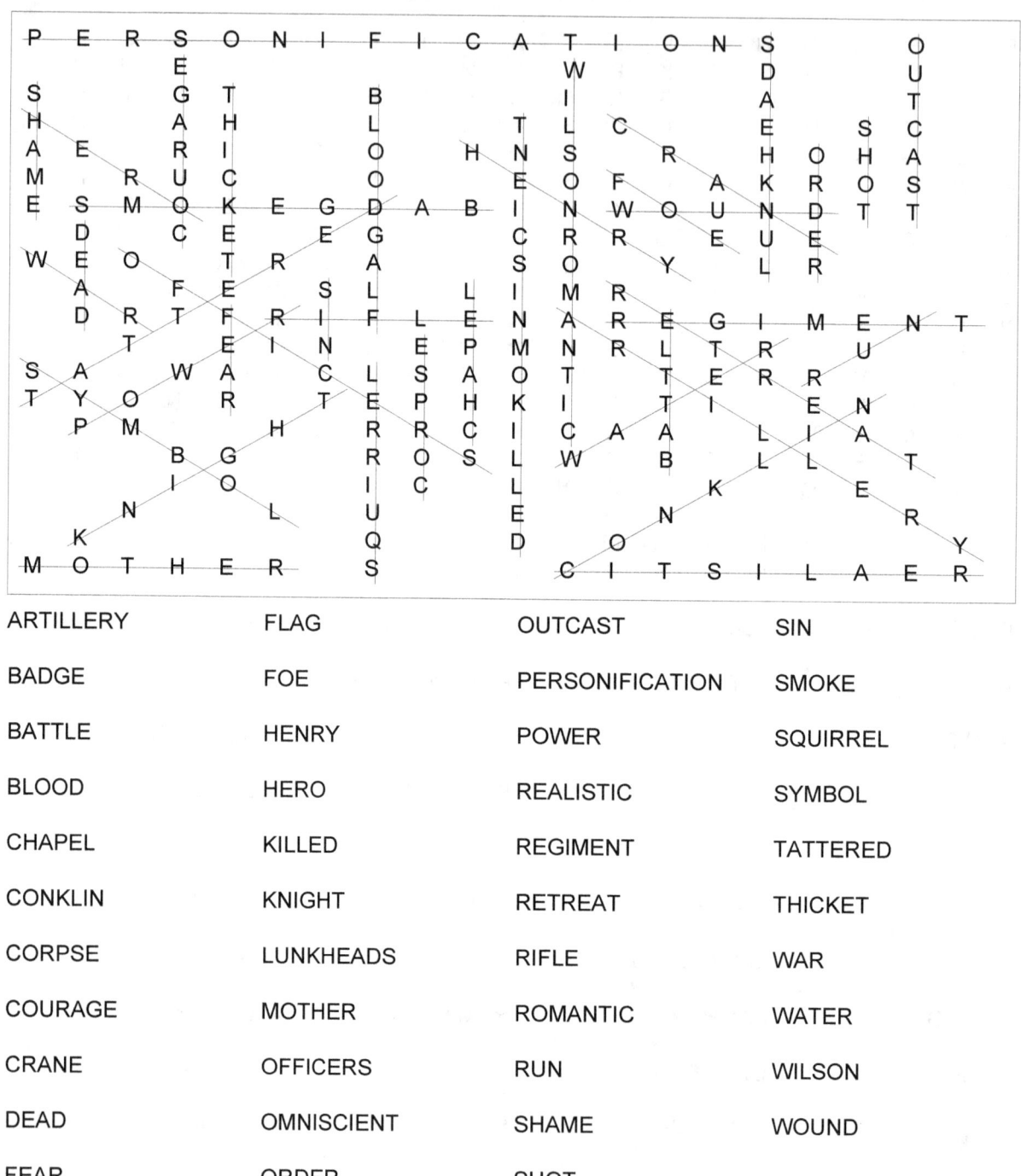

ARTILLERY	FLAG	OUTCAST	SIN
BADGE	FOE	PERSONIFICATION	SMOKE
BATTLE	HENRY	POWER	SQUIRREL
BLOOD	HERO	REALISTIC	SYMBOL
CHAPEL	KILLED	REGIMENT	TATTERED
CONKLIN	KNIGHT	RETREAT	THICKET
CORPSE	LUNKHEADS	RIFLE	WAR
COURAGE	MOTHER	ROMANTIC	WATER
CRANE	OFFICERS	RUN	WILSON
DEAD	OMNISCIENT	SHAME	WOUND
FEAR	ORDER	SHOT	

Red Badge of Courage Crossword 1

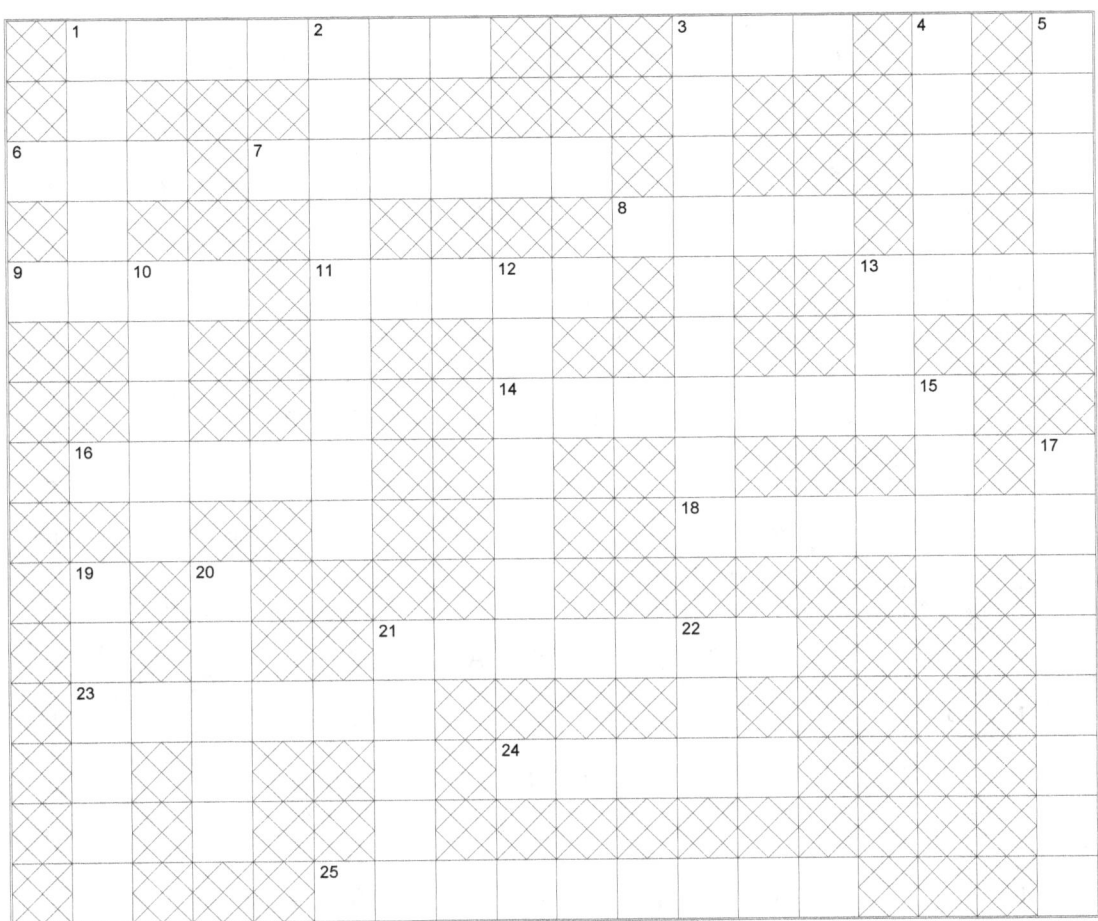

Across
1. Tall soldier Jim
3. Henry's first concern was that he would ____ from battle.
6. The Civil ____
7. He had slept and awakening had found himself a ____.
8. Henry carried it into battle
9. One others exalt because of his deeds
11. Soldier Fleming
13. Feeling of being afraid
14. Man Henry left in the man's time of need: ____ soldier
16. Red fluid on soldiers' bandages
18. Bravery
21. Henry felt like a mental ____.
23. Henry should not shirk his duty because of her.
24. Injury; where a bullet may have hit, for example
25. The big guns; cannon, for example

Down
1. Author Stephen
2. What the soldiers called their inept commanders
3. Seeing things as they really are; not romantic
4. Red ____ of Courage
5. Henry endowed the flag with this because no harm could come to it.
10. Long gun
12. Go backward; lose ground in battle
13. Enemy
15. Henry wished he were ____, so he wouldn't have to face his embarrassing retreat.
17. Military unit consisting of Battalion, et al.
19. Something that stands for something else
20. Liquid in soldiers' canteens
21. Command soldiers follow
22. Henry's ____ was deserting the tattered soldier.

Red Badge of Courage Crossword 1 Answer Key

	1 C	O	N	K	L	I	N			3 R	U	N		4 B		5 P
	R				U					E				A		O
6 W	A	R		7 K	N	I	G	H	T	A				D		W
	N				K				8 F	L	A	G		G		E
9 H	E	10 R	O		11 H	E	N	12 R	Y				13 F	E	A	R
		I			E			E		S			O			
		F			A		14 T	A	T	T	E	R	E	D	15 D		17 R
	16 B	L	O	O	D			R		I					E		R
		E			S			E		18 C	O	U	R	A	G	E
19 S		20 W						A							D		G
Y		A				21 O	U	T	C	22 A	S	T					I
23 M	O	T	H	E	R					S							M
B		E				24 W	O	U	N	D							E
O		R				E											N
L				25 A	R	T	I	L	L	E	R	Y					T

Across
1. Tall soldier Jim
3. Henry's first concern was that he would ____ from battle.
6. The Civil ____
7. He had slept and awakening had found himself a ____.
8. Henry carried it into battle
9. One others exalt because of his deeds
11. Soldier Fleming
13. Feeling of being afraid
14. Man Henry left in the man's time of need: ____ soldier
16. Red fluid on soldiers' bandages
18. Bravery
21. Henry felt like a mental ____.
23. Henry should not shirk his duty because of her.
24. Injury; where a bullet may have hit, for example
25. The big guns; cannon, for example

Down
1. Author Stephen
2. What the soldiers called their inept commanders
3. Seeing things as they really are; not romantic
4. Red ____ of Courage
5. Henry endowed the flag with this because no harm could come to it.
10. Long gun
12. Go backward; lose ground in battle
13. Enemy
15. Henry wished he were ____, so he wouldn't have to face his embarrassing retreat.
17. Military unit consisting of Battalion, et al.
19. Something that stands for something else
20. Liquid in soldiers' canteens
21. Command soldiers follow
22. Henry's ____ was deserting the tattered soldier.

Red Badge of Courage Crossword 2

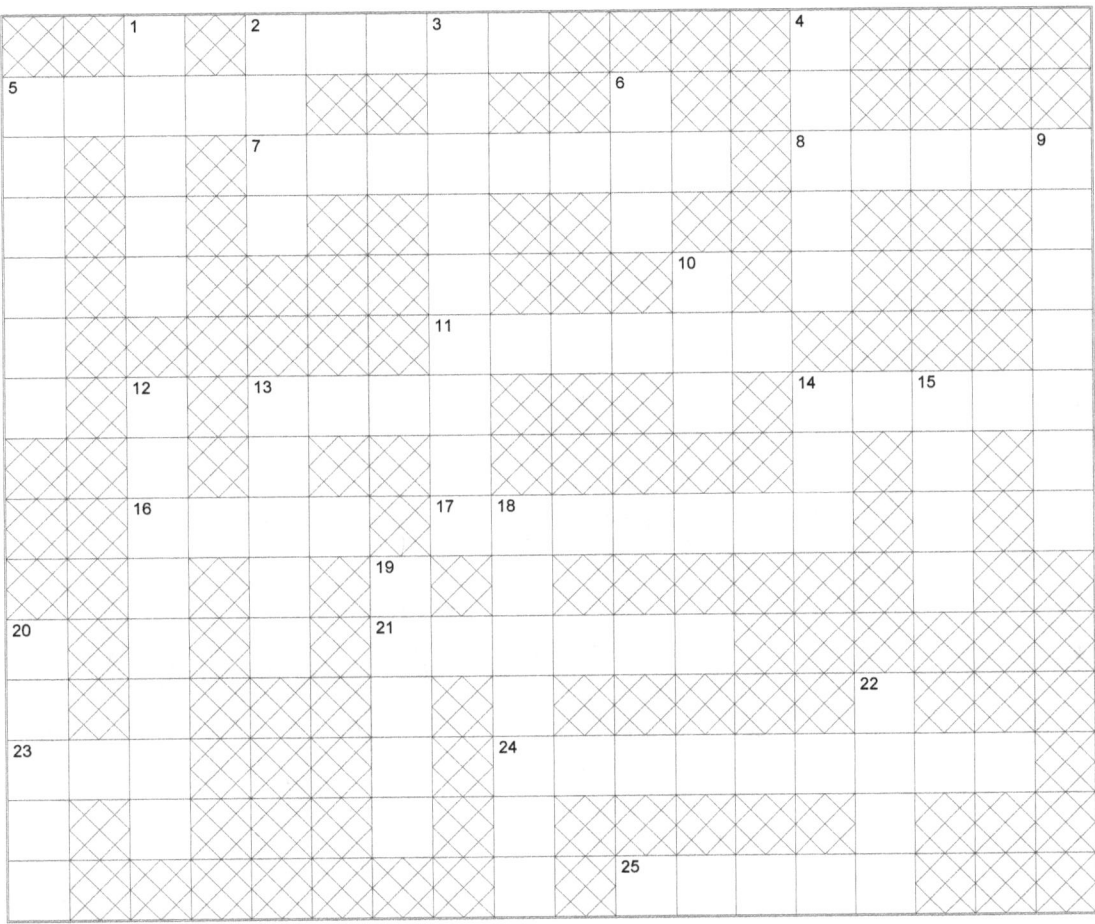

Across
2. Soldier Fleming
5. Author Stephen
7. Unrealistic; seeing things rosier than they really are
8. Command soldiers follow
11. Something that stands for something else
13. Henry lies about his wound and says he was _____.
14. Long gun
16. Henry carried it into battle
17. Tall soldier Jim
21. Henry should not shirk his duty because of her.
23. The Civil ____
24. The big guns; cannon, for example
25. Injury; where a bullet may have hit, for example

Down
1. Red ____ of Courage
2. One others exalt because of his deeds
3. Seeing things as they really are; not romantic
4. Red fluid on soldiers' bandages
5. Place in forest where Henry came upon the dead soldier
6. Henry's ____ was deserting the tattered soldier.
9. Go backward; lose ground in battle
10. Enemy
12. They give commands.
13. The retreat of the mule drivers was a march of ____ to Henry.
14. Henry's first concern was that he would ____ from battle.
15. Feeling of being afraid
18. Henry felt like a mental ____.
19. Firing gunpowder caused this, which made seeing difficult.
20. Henry endowed the flag with this because no harm could come to it.
22. Henry wished he were ____, so he wouldn't have to face his embarrassing retreat.

39
Copyrighted

Red Badge of Courage Crossword 2 Answer Key

		1 B		2 H	E	N	3 R	Y			4 B		
5 C	R	A	N	E			E			6 S	L		
H		D		7 R	O	M	A	N	T	I	C	8 O	R	D	E	9 R
A		G		O			L			N		O				E
P		E					I			10 F		D				T
E						11 S	Y	M	B	O	L					R
L		12 O		13 S	H	O	T			E		14 R	I	15 F	L	E
		F		H			I					U		E		A
		16 F	L	A	G		17 C	18 O	N	K	L	I	N		A		T
		I		M		19 S		U						R
20 P		C		E		21 M	O	T	H	E	R		
O		E				O		C						22 D
23 W	A	R				K		24 A	R	T	I	L	L	E	R	Y
E		S				E		S						A
R						T		25 W	O	U	N	D

Across
2. Soldier Fleming
5. Author Stephen
7. Unrealistic; seeing things rosier than they really are
8. Command soldiers follow
11. Something that stands for something else
13. Henry lies about his wound and says he was _____.
14. Long gun
16. Henry carried it into battle
17. Tall soldier Jim
21. Henry should not shirk his duty because of her.
23. The Civil ____
24. The big guns; cannon, for example
25. Injury; where a bullet may have hit, for example

Down
1. Red ____ of Courage
2. One others exalt because of his deeds
3. Seeing things as they really are; not romantic
4. Red fluid on soldiers' bandages
5. Place in forest where Henry came upon the dead soldier
6. Henry's ____ was deserting the tattered soldier.
9. Go backward; lose ground in battle
10. Enemy
12. They give commands.
13. The retreat of the mule drivers was a march of ____ to Henry.
14. Henry's first concern was that he would ____ from battle.
15. Feeling of being afraid
18. Henry felt like a mental ____.
19. Firing gunpowder caused this, which made seeing difficult.
20. Henry endowed the flag with this because no harm could come to it.
22. Henry wished he were ____, so he wouldn't have to face his embarrassing retreat.

Red Badge of Courage Crossword 3

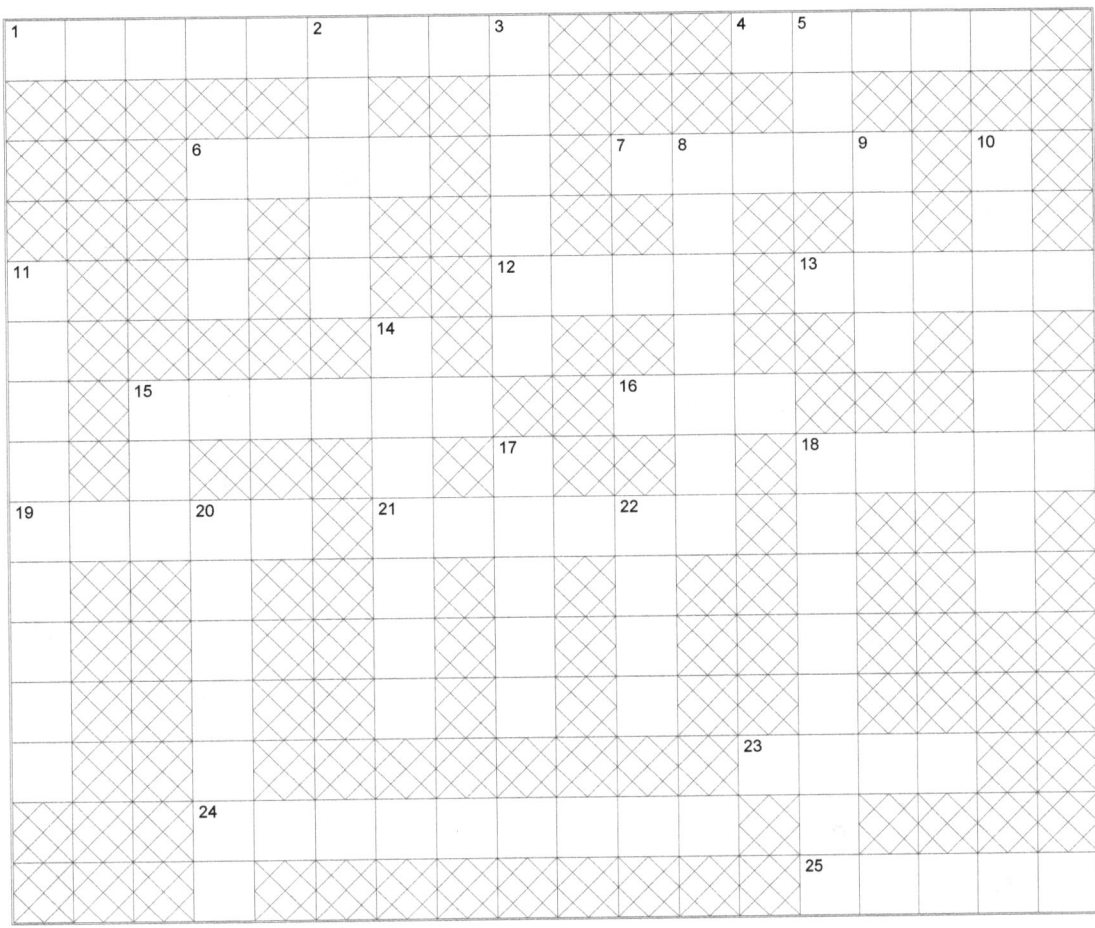

Across
1. Seeing things as they really are; not romantic
4. Author Stephen
6. Henry carried it into battle
7. Injury; where a bullet may have hit, for example
12. Henry lies about his wound and says he was _____.
13. Red ____ of Courage
15. Something that stands for something else
16. The Civil ____
18. Command soldiers follow
19. Soldier Fleming
21. He had slept and awakening had found himself a ____.
23. Feeling of being afraid
24. The big guns; cannon, for example
25. Firing gunpowder caused this, which made seeing difficult.

Down
2. The retreat of the mule drivers was a march of ____ to Henry.
3. Dead body
5. Henry's first concern was that he would ____ from battle.
6. Enemy
8. Henry felt like a mental ____.
9. Henry wished he were ____, so he wouldn't have to face his embarrassing retreat.
10. Military unit consisting of Battalion, et al.
11. What the soldiers called their inept commanders
14. Tall soldier Jim
15. Henry's ____ was deserting the tattered soldier.
17. Long gun
18. They give commands.
20. Go backward; lose ground in battle
22. One others exalt because of his deeds

Red Badge of Courage Crossword 3 Answer Key

	1 R	E	A	L	I	2 S	T	I	3 C			4 C	5 R	A	N	E	
						H			O				U				
			6 F	L	A	G			R		7 W	8 O	U	N	9 D		10 R
			O		M				P			U			E		E
11 L			E		E			12 S	H	O	T			13 B	A	D	G	E
U						14 C		E				C			D		I
N		15 S	Y	M	B	O	L			16 W	A	R					M
K		I				N		17 R				S		18 O	R	D	E	R
19 H	E	20 N	R	Y		21 K	N	I	G	H	22 T			F			N
E		E				L		F			E			F			T
A		T				I		L			R			I			
D		R				N		E			R			C			
S		E									O		23 F	E	A	R	
		24 A	R	T	I	L	L	E	R	Y			R				
		T										25 S	M	O	K	E

Across

1. Seeing things as they really are; not romantic
4. Author Stephen
6. Henry carried it into battle
7. Injury; where a bullet may have hit, for example
12. Henry lies about his wound and says he was _____.
13. Red ____ of Courage
15. Something that stands for something else
16. The Civil ____
18. Command soldiers follow
19. Soldier Fleming
21. He had slept and awakening had found himself a ____.
23. Feeling of being afraid
24. The big guns; cannon, for example
25. Firing gunpowder caused this, which made seeing difficult.

Down

2. The retreat of the mule drivers was a march of ____ to Henry.
3. Dead body
5. Henry's first concern was that he would ____ from battle.
6. Enemy
8. Henry felt like a mental ____.
9. Henry wished he were ____, so he wouldn't have to face his embarrassing retreat.
10. Military unit consisting of Battalion, et al.
11. What the soldiers called their inept commanders
14. Tall soldier Jim
15. Henry's ____ was deserting the tattered soldier.
17. Long gun
18. They give commands.
20. Go backward; lose ground in battle
22. One others exalt because of his deeds

Red Badge of Courage Crossword 4

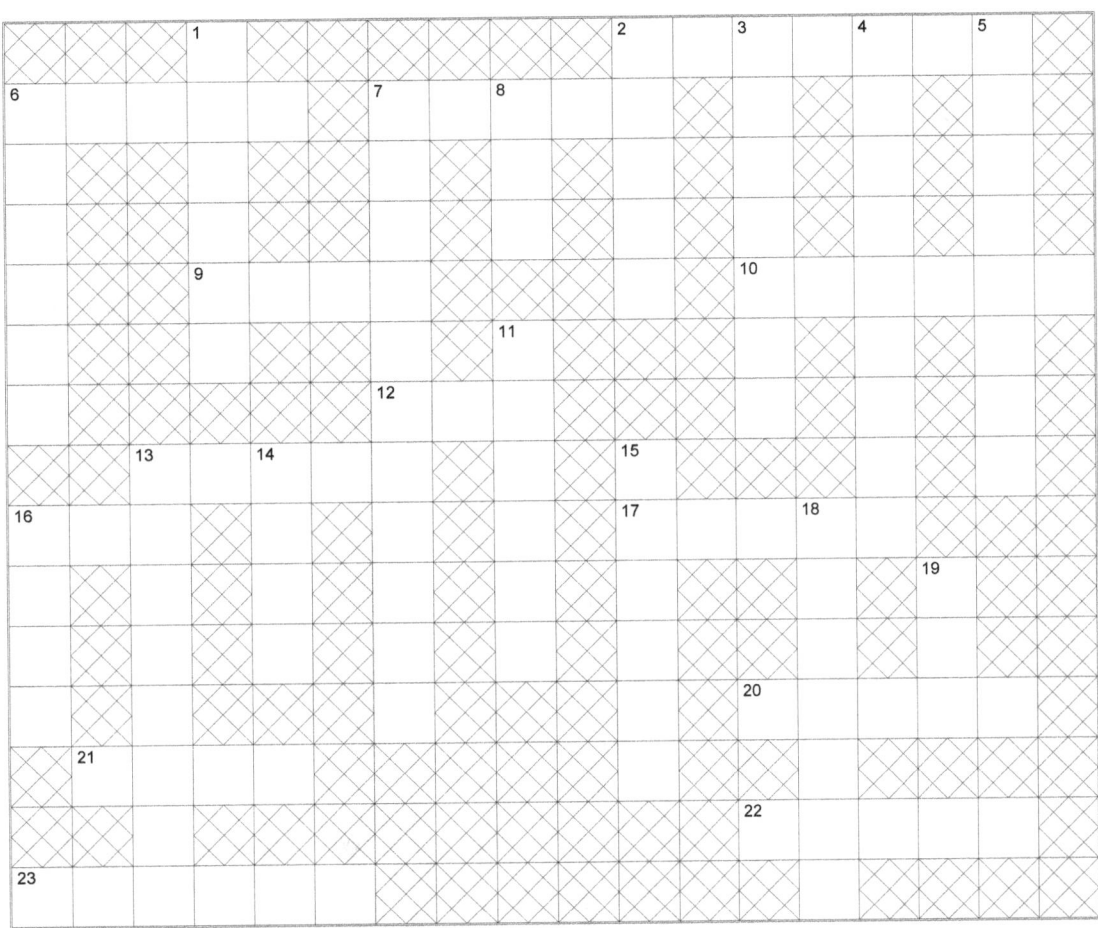

Across

2. Henry felt like a mental ____.
6. Red fluid on soldiers' bandages
7. Henry endowed the flag with this because no harm could come to it.
9. Henry lies about his wound and says he was ____.
10. Henry thought it would be better to get ____ directly.
12. Henry's first concern was that he would ____ from battle.
13. Long gun
16. Enemy
17. Soldier Fleming
20. Author Stephen
21. Henry wished he were ____, so he wouldn't have to face his embarrassing retreat.
22. Liquid in soldiers' canteens
23. Henry should not shirk his duty because of her.

Down

1. Dead body
2. Command soldiers follow
3. Dense growth of shrubs and underbrush
4. The big guns; cannon, for example
5. Man Henry left in the man's time of need: ____ soldier
6. An episode of fighting
7. The officers neglected to stand in ____ attitudes.
8. The Civil ____
11. He had slept and awakening had found himself a ____.
13. Military unit consisting of Battalion, et al.
14. Feeling of being afraid
15. Place in forest where Henry came upon the dead soldier
16. Henry carried it into battle
18. Go backward; lose ground in battle
19. Henry's ____ was deserting the tattered soldier.

Red Badge of Courage Crossword 4 Answer Key

			1 C					2 O	3 U	T	4 C	A	5 T	
6 B	L	O	O	D		7 P	8 O	W	E	R		H		R	A
A		R		I		A		D			I		T	T
T		P		C		R		E			C		I	T
T		9 S	H	O	T			R		10 K	I	L	L	E	D
L		E		U	11 K				E		L		R
E			12 R	U	N				T		E		E
	13 R	14 I	F	L	E		15 C			R		D
16 F	O	E		E	S		G		17 H	E	N	18 R	Y
L		G		A	Q		H		A			E		19 S
A		I		R	U		T		P			T		I
G		M			E				20 E	C	R	A	N	E
	21 D	E	A	D					L			E	
	N									22 W	A	T	E	R
23 M	O	T	H	E	R					T			

Across
2. Henry felt like a mental ____.
6. Red fluid on soldiers' bandages
7. Henry endowed the flag with this because no harm could come to it.
9. Henry lies about his wound and says he was _____.
10. Henry thought it would be better to get ____ directly.
12. Henry's first concern was that he would ____ from battle.
13. Long gun
16. Enemy
17. Soldier Fleming
20. Author Stephen
21. Henry wished he were ____, so he wouldn't have to face his embarrassing retreat.
22. Liquid in soldiers' canteens
23. Henry should not shirk his duty because of her.

Down
1. Dead body
2. Command soldiers follow
3. Dense growth of shrubs and underbrush
4. The big guns; cannon, for example
5. Man Henry left in the man's time of need: ____ soldier
6. An episode of fighting
7. The officers neglected to stand in ____ attitudes.
8. The Civil ____
11. He had slept and awakening had found himself a ____.
13. Military unit consisting of Battalion, et al.
14. Feeling of being afraid
15. Place in forest where Henry came upon the dead soldier
16. Henry carried it into battle
18. Go backward; lose ground in battle
19. Henry's ____ was deserting the tattered soldier.

Red Badge of Courage

BADGE	BLOOD	REALISTIC	BATTLE	DEAD
KILLED	SYMBOL	REGIMENT	KNIGHT	WAR
PICTURESQUE	CONKLIN	FREE SPACE	LUNKHEADS	SQUIRREL
ORDER	OFFICERS	WATER	THICKET	POWER
SIN	OMNISCIENT	PERSONIFICATION	FEAR	SMOKE

Red Badge of Courage

RIFLE	MOTHER	FOE	COURAGE	HERO
SHOT	ARTILLERY	HENRY	CORPSE	RETREAT
SHAME	CRANE	FREE SPACE	TATTERED	RUN
WOUND	FLAG	CHAPEL	ROMANTIC	SMOKE
FEAR	PERSONIFICATION	OMNISCIENT	SIN	POWER

Red Badge of Courage

PERSONIFICATION	SHAME	TATTERED	WATER	SMOKE
ROMANTIC	CORPSE	ORDER	KILLED	OUTCAST
RETREAT	WOUND	FREE SPACE	MOTHER	CHAPEL
POWER	BATTLE	PICTURESQUE	REALISTIC	DEAD
HENRY	FEAR	THICKET	FLAG	WILSON

Red Badge of Courage

OFFICERS	BLOOD	RIFLE	FOE	KNIGHT
CRANE	SQUIRREL	OMNISCIENT	CONKLIN	SHOT
WAR	HERO	FREE SPACE	SYMBOL	LUNKHEADS
REGIMENT	RUN	ARTILLERY	COURAGE	WILSON
FLAG	THICKET	FEAR	HENRY	DEAD

Red Badge of Courage

WAR	LUNKHEADS	WATER	BADGE	CORPSE
RIFLE	TATTERED	POWER	ROMANTIC	HENRY
OUTCAST	RUN	FREE SPACE	FLAG	DEAD
SHOT	ARTILLERY	ORDER	MOTHER	CHAPEL
HERO	RETREAT	PICTURESQUE	COURAGE	WOUND

Red Badge of Courage

OFFICERS	PERSONIFICATION	FOE	REALISTIC	WILSON
THICKET	FEAR	SMOKE	BATTLE	SYMBOL
REGIMENT	BLOOD	FREE SPACE	KNIGHT	SIN
SHAME	CONKLIN	OMNISCIENT	KILLED	WOUND
COURAGE	PICTURESQUE	RETREAT	HERO	CHAPEL

Red Badge of Courage

REGIMENT	SMOKE	POWER	PERSONIFICATION	SHOT
THICKET	ROMANTIC	BLOOD	KNIGHT	CHAPEL
MOTHER	RETREAT	FREE SPACE	TATTERED	FEAR
SYMBOL	HENRY	DEAD	WOUND	REALISTIC
WILSON	BADGE	PICTURESQUE	CORPSE	COURAGE

Red Badge of Courage

CONKLIN	KILLED	SQUIRREL	HERO	SIN
ORDER	WATER	OUTCAST	FOE	RIFLE
ARTILLERY	FLAG	FREE SPACE	CRANE	LUNKHEADS
RUN	OFFICERS	BATTLE	WAR	COURAGE
CORPSE	PICTURESQUE	BADGE	WILSON	REALISTIC

Red Badge of Courage

COURAGE	RUN	FOE	ROMANTIC	POWER
KNIGHT	WILSON	WAR	THICKET	CORPSE
LUNKHEADS	HERO	FREE SPACE	SIN	CRANE
HENRY	BATTLE	KILLED	WATER	FLAG
SHAME	BADGE	ARTILLERY	RIFLE	CHAPEL

Red Badge of Courage

SHOT	OMNISCIENT	SMOKE	REGIMENT	TATTERED
OFFICERS	WOUND	DEAD	CONKLIN	OUTCAST
PERSONIFICATION	SYMBOL	FREE SPACE	PICTURESQUE	SQUIRREL
ORDER	FEAR	MOTHER	REALISTIC	CHAPEL
RIFLE	ARTILLERY	BADGE	SHAME	FLAG

Red Badge of Courage

SHOT	ORDER	RIFLE	RETREAT	SHAME
RUN	THICKET	WAR	WOUND	TATTERED
REGIMENT	FLAG	FREE SPACE	KNIGHT	BADGE
HERO	FOE	BLOOD	FEAR	PICTURESQUE
ARTILLERY	WATER	SMOKE	CHAPEL	REALISTIC

Red Badge of Courage

CRANE	SYMBOL	KILLED	WILSON	LUNKHEADS
PERSONIFICATION	SIN	MOTHER	SQUIRREL	COURAGE
OFFICERS	HENRY	FREE SPACE	CORPSE	DEAD
ROMANTIC	BATTLE	POWER	OUTCAST	REALISTIC
CHAPEL	SMOKE	WATER	ARTILLERY	PICTURESQUE

Red Badge of Courage

FLAG	FOE	SMOKE	OUTCAST	HENRY
LUNKHEADS	PERSONIFICATION	SHAME	CRANE	PICTURESQUE
SIN	REALISTIC	FREE SPACE	KILLED	WAR
WATER	RUN	CORPSE	WOUND	CHAPEL
POWER	ARTILLERY	HERO	COURAGE	OMNISCIENT

Red Badge of Courage

BATTLE	DEAD	FEAR	BADGE	KNIGHT
ORDER	CONKLIN	SYMBOL	OFFICERS	ROMANTIC
SHOT	BLOOD	FREE SPACE	MOTHER	RIFLE
RETREAT	SQUIRREL	TATTERED	REGIMENT	OMNISCIENT
COURAGE	HERO	ARTILLERY	POWER	CHAPEL

Red Badge of Courage

WATER	SYMBOL	ARTILLERY	ROMANTIC	OFFICERS
FEAR	PERSONIFICATION	KNIGHT	BATTLE	REGIMENT
CORPSE	CRANE	FREE SPACE	REALISTIC	SQUIRREL
COURAGE	BLOOD	WOUND	FOE	HENRY
SIN	ORDER	LUNKHEADS	RUN	SHAME

Red Badge of Courage

POWER	HERO	KILLED	SHOT	MOTHER
OMNISCIENT	WAR	BADGE	DEAD	CONKLIN
PICTURESQUE	RETREAT	FREE SPACE	SMOKE	WILSON
FLAG	THICKET	TATTERED	OUTCAST	SHAME
RUN	LUNKHEADS	ORDER	SIN	HENRY

Red Badge of Courage

TATTERED	BADGE	FEAR	CORPSE	SIN
WILSON	THICKET	BATTLE	REALISTIC	ORDER
PICTURESQUE	CHAPEL	FREE SPACE	SQUIRREL	HENRY
BLOOD	REGIMENT	WATER	RIFLE	RUN
POWER	RETREAT	FOE	COURAGE	HERO

Red Badge of Courage

OMNISCIENT	SHAME	CRANE	KILLED	CONKLIN
DEAD	LUNKHEADS	WOUND	PERSONIFICATION	ARTILLERY
MOTHER	FLAG	FREE SPACE	OUTCAST	SYMBOL
ROMANTIC	WAR	SHOT	KNIGHT	HERO
COURAGE	FOE	RETREAT	POWER	RUN

Red Badge of Courage

CHAPEL	FOE	CRANE	WAR	PERSONIFICATION
HERO	ORDER	WOUND	CONKLIN	REGIMENT
BATTLE	FEAR	FREE SPACE	ROMANTIC	OFFICERS
OUTCAST	BADGE	RUN	WILSON	ARTILLERY
SHOT	SIN	MOTHER	REALISTIC	SQUIRREL

Red Badge of Courage

RIFLE	WATER	THICKET	KNIGHT	KILLED
DEAD	SHAME	POWER	OMNISCIENT	SYMBOL
LUNKHEADS	COURAGE	FREE SPACE	CORPSE	RETREAT
BLOOD	FLAG	PICTURESQUE	TATTERED	SQUIRREL
REALISTIC	MOTHER	SIN	SHOT	ARTILLERY

Red Badge of Courage

SIN	SYMBOL	HENRY	OMNISCIENT	SMOKE
CONKLIN	KNIGHT	COURAGE	OFFICERS	WOUND
FOE	ORDER	FREE SPACE	CRANE	TATTERED
KILLED	SQUIRREL	DEAD	MOTHER	RETREAT
REALISTIC	ROMANTIC	RIFLE	OUTCAST	WAR

Red Badge of Courage

WILSON	BATTLE	FLAG	CHAPEL	BADGE
SHOT	PICTURESQUE	THICKET	WATER	POWER
HERO	CORPSE	FREE SPACE	REGIMENT	SHAME
FEAR	ARTILLERY	BLOOD	RUN	WAR
OUTCAST	RIFLE	ROMANTIC	REALISTIC	RETREAT

Red Badge of Courage

ORDER	KILLED	ARTILLERY	REALISTIC	HERO
REGIMENT	SMOKE	RETREAT	WAR	SYMBOL
POWER	KNIGHT	FREE SPACE	OMNISCIENT	FLAG
TATTERED	WOUND	SHAME	FEAR	FOE
ROMANTIC	CORPSE	OFFICERS	WATER	RUN

Red Badge of Courage

OUTCAST	BADGE	CONKLIN	SHOT	LUNKHEADS
BLOOD	DEAD	BATTLE	RIFLE	SIN
SQUIRREL	CHAPEL	FREE SPACE	WILSON	MOTHER
HENRY	COURAGE	CRANE	PERSONIFICATION	RUN
WATER	OFFICERS	CORPSE	ROMANTIC	FOE

Red Badge of Courage

REALISTIC	CRANE	OUTCAST	COURAGE	DEAD
ROMANTIC	SMOKE	BADGE	THICKET	RIFLE
FLAG	WILSON	FREE SPACE	CHAPEL	ARTILLERY
POWER	PERSONIFICATION	FOE	TATTERED	SIN
BLOOD	KNIGHT	SQUIRREL	RETREAT	CORPSE

Red Badge of Courage

REGIMENT	HERO	OMNISCIENT	SYMBOL	SHAME
SHOT	BATTLE	HENRY	WAR	OFFICERS
RUN	MOTHER	FREE SPACE	CONKLIN	LUNKHEADS
FEAR	WATER	KILLED	PICTURESQUE	CORPSE
RETREAT	SQUIRREL	KNIGHT	BLOOD	SIN

Red Badge of Courage

CORPSE	SQUIRREL	BLOOD	RETREAT	OFFICERS
SIN	OUTCAST	PERSONIFICATION	COURAGE	THICKET
REALISTIC	ROMANTIC	FREE SPACE	DEAD	ARTILLERY
HERO	CRANE	CHAPEL	RUN	SYMBOL
SHAME	WATER	KILLED	KNIGHT	FOE

Red Badge of Courage

FEAR	WAR	ORDER	REGIMENT	TATTERED
POWER	MOTHER	CONKLIN	OMNISCIENT	RIFLE
BATTLE	SMOKE	FREE SPACE	HENRY	PICTURESQUE
WOUND	FLAG	BADGE	LUNKHEADS	FOE
KNIGHT	KILLED	WATER	SHAME	SYMBOL

Red Badge of Courage

SHAME	REALISTIC	SQUIRREL	OUTCAST	POWER
ORDER	RUN	ROMANTIC	CONKLIN	CRANE
RETREAT	REGIMENT	FREE SPACE	BLOOD	WILSON
OFFICERS	WOUND	MOTHER	HERO	BADGE
PERSONIFICATION	KILLED	WAR	PICTURESQUE	LUNKHEADS

Red Badge of Courage

COURAGE	SHOT	THICKET	BATTLE	DEAD
SIN	WATER	RIFLE	HENRY	KNIGHT
CORPSE	TATTERED	FREE SPACE	ARTILLERY	CHAPEL
SMOKE	OMNISCIENT	FLAG	FOE	LUNKHEADS
PICTURESQUE	WAR	KILLED	PERSONIFICATION	BADGE

Red Badge of Courage

RUN	WATER	ARTILLERY	CRANE	SMOKE
POWER	THICKET	CORPSE	FLAG	ROMANTIC
MOTHER	CHAPEL	FREE SPACE	SYMBOL	FEAR
SHOT	TATTERED	CONKLIN	OMNISCIENT	WAR
RIFLE	SHAME	BATTLE	OFFICERS	PICTURESQUE

Red Badge of Courage

COURAGE	LUNKHEADS	DEAD	OUTCAST	REALISTIC
BADGE	BLOOD	ORDER	PERSONIFICATION	WOUND
SIN	HENRY	FREE SPACE	KNIGHT	HERO
KILLED	WILSON	REGIMENT	FOE	PICTURESQUE
OFFICERS	BATTLE	SHAME	RIFLE	WAR

Red Badge of Courage Vocabulary Word List

No.	Word	Clue/Definition
1.	ABJECT	Wretched; of the most contemptible kind
2.	AGUE	A recurrent chill or fit of shivering
3.	ALTERCATION	Heating or noisy quarrel
4.	ANNIHILATED	Wiped out; destroyed completely
5.	AUDACIOUS	Arrogantly insolent
6.	BEDRAGGLED	Made wet and limp
7.	BLITHE	Cheerful; casual; carefree
8.	CHAOS	Total disorder or confusion
9.	CONDESCENSION	The act of coming down voluntarily to the level of inferiors
10.	DAUNTLESS	Fearless; bold
11.	DELIRIUM	Temporary mental confusion
12.	DENOTED	Marked; indicated; signified
13.	DENUNCIATION	An open condemnation or censure
14.	DESPONDENT	Feeling disheartened or dejected
15.	DISCERNED	Detected; perceived
16.	DISCONCERTED	Lacking self-composure
17.	ELATION	Exalted feeling arising from a sense of triumph, power or relief
18.	EXASPERATION	The state of extremely annoyed or irritated
19.	FACETIOUS	Humorous and flippant; playfully jocular
20.	FORMIDABLE	Arousing fear or dread; awesome; difficult to overtake
21.	HEEDLESS	Paying little or no attention; unmindful
22.	IMPENDING	Likely to happen soon
23.	IMPETUS	Impelling force; impulse; stimulus
24.	IMPRECATIONS	Curses
25.	INDIGNANTLY	With an anger aroused by something unjust
26.	INTERMINABLE	Endless
27.	LUDICROUS	Laughable because of obvious absurdity or incongruity
28.	MALEDICTION	A curse or slander
29.	MOROSE	Melancholy; gloomy; ill-humored
30.	OBDURATE	Intractable; not giving in
31.	OBLIGED	Caused to do something
32.	OBSCURITY	The condition of being unknown
33.	OMINOUS	Portentous; foreboding
34.	ORBS	Eyes
35.	PERFUNCTORY	Acting with little interest or care
36.	PLACIDLY	Outwardly calm or composed; complacent
37.	PONDEROUS	Massive
38.	PRODIGIOUS	Enormous, extraordinary; marvelous
39.	PROXIMITY	Closeness
40.	RELIANCE	Confidence; dependence; trust
41.	REPOSE	Rest
42.	REPROOF	Reprimand
43.	SARDONIC	Mocking; cynical
44.	SINUOUS	Winding
45.	SMITTEN	Afflicted
46.	SPECTER	Ghost; phantasm
47.	SULLEN	Morose, sulky
48.	VANQUISHED	Defeated; overcome
49.	VINDICATION	The evidence or argument that justifies an act

Red Badge of Courage Vocabulary Fill In The Blanks 1

_____ 1. Defeated; overcome

_____ 2. Impelling force; impulse; stimulus

_____ 3. Feeling disheartened or dejected

_____ 4. Reprimand

_____ 5. Wretched; of the most contemptible kind

_____ 6. Wiped out; destroyed completely

_____ 7. Eyes

_____ 8. The condition of being unknown

_____ 9. Outwardly calm or composed; complacent

_____ 10. Exalted feeling arising from a sense of triumph, power or relief

_____ 11. Fearless; bold

_____ 12. Humorous and flippant; playfully jocular

_____ 13. Laughable because of obvious absurdity or incongruity

_____ 14. Caused to do something

_____ 15. Mocking; cynical

_____ 16. Paying little or no attention; unmindful

_____ 17. Endless

_____ 18. Acting with little interest or care

_____ 19. Ghost; phantasm

_____ 20. Arrogantly insolent

Red Badge of Courage Vocabulary Fill In The Blanks 1 Answer Key

VANQUISHED	1. Defeated; overcome
IMPETUS	2. Impelling force; impulse; stimulus
DESPONDENT	3. Feeling disheartened or dejected
REPROOF	4. Reprimand
ABJECT	5. Wretched; of the most contemptible kind
ANNIHILATED	6. Wiped out; destroyed completely
ORBS	7. Eyes
OBSCURITY	8. The condition of being unknown
PLACIDLY	9. Outwardly calm or composed; complacent
ELATION	10. Exalted feeling arising from a sense of triumph, power or relief
DAUNTLESS	11. Fearless; bold
FACETIOUS	12. Humorous and flippant; playfully jocular
LUDICROUS	13. Laughable because of obvious absurdity or incongruity
OBLIGED	14. Caused to do something
SARDONIC	15. Mocking; cynical
HEEDLESS	16. Paying little or no attention; unmindful
INTERMINABLE	17. Endless
PERFUNCTORY	18. Acting with little interest or care
SPECTER	19. Ghost; phantasm
AUDACIOUS	20. Arrogantly insolent

Red Badge of Courage Vocabulary Fill In The Blanks 2

_____ 1. Arousing fear or dread; awesome; difficult to overtake

_____ 2. Ghost; phantasm

_____ 3. Eyes

_____ 4. Humorous and flippant; playfully jocular

_____ 5. Morose, sulky

_____ 6. The condition of being unknown

_____ 7. The act of coming down voluntarily to the level of inferiors

_____ 8. Mocking; cynical

_____ 9. Temporary mental confusion

_____ 10. Total disorder or confusion

_____ 11. Exalted feeling arising from a sense of triumph, power or relief

_____ 12. Feeling disheartened or dejected

_____ 13. Defeated; overcome

_____ 14. Endless

_____ 15. Winding

_____ 16. Arrogantly insolent

_____ 17. The evidence or argument that justifies an act

_____ 18. Cheerful; casual; carefree

_____ 19. Curses

_____ 20. Paying little or no attention; unmindful

Red Badge of Courage Vocabulary Fill In The Blanks 2 Answer Key

FORMIDABLE	1. Arousing fear or dread; awesome; difficult to overtake
SPECTER	2. Ghost; phantasm
ORBS	3. Eyes
FACETIOUS	4. Humorous and flippant; playfully jocular
SULLEN	5. Morose, sulky
OBSCURITY	6. The condition of being unknown
CONDESCENSION	7. The act of coming down voluntarily to the level of inferiors
SARDONIC	8. Mocking; cynical
DELIRIUM	9. Temporary mental confusion
CHAOS	10. Total disorder or confusion
ELATION	11. Exalted feeling arising from a sense of triumph, power or relief
DESPONDENT	12. Feeling disheartened or dejected
VANQUISHED	13. Defeated; overcome
INTERMINABLE	14. Endless
SINUOUS	15. Winding
AUDACIOUS	16. Arrogantly insolent
VINDICATION	17. The evidence or argument that justifies an act
BLITHE	18. Cheerful; casual; carefree
IMPRECATIONS	19. Curses
HEEDLESS	20. Paying little or no attention; unmindful

Red Badge of Courage Vocabulary Fill In The Blanks 3

_____ 1. Defeated; overcome

_____ 2. The evidence or argument that justifies an act

_____ 3. Confidence; dependence; trust

_____ 4. Wiped out; destroyed completely

_____ 5. Eyes

_____ 6. Cheerful; casual; carefree

_____ 7. Lacking self-composure

_____ 8. Exalted feeling arising from a sense of triumph, power or relief

_____ 9. Intractable; not giving in

_____ 10. Fearless; bold

_____ 11. The state of extremely annoyed or irritated

_____ 12. Enormous, extraordinary; marvelous

_____ 13. Paying little or no attention; unmindful

_____ 14. Afflicted

_____ 15. Arrogantly insolent

_____ 16. Feeling disheartened or dejected

_____ 17. Melancholy; gloomy; ill-humored

_____ 18. A recurrent chill or fit of shivering

_____ 19. The act of coming down voluntarily to the level of inferiors

_____ 20. Curses

Red Badge of Courage Vocabulary Fill In The Blanks 3 Answer Key

VANQUISHED	1. Defeated; overcome
VINDICATION	2. The evidence or argument that justifies an act
RELIANCE	3. Confidence; dependence; trust
ANNIHILATED	4. Wiped out; destroyed completely
ORBS	5. Eyes
BLITHE	6. Cheerful; casual; carefree
DISCONCERTED	7. Lacking self-composure
ELATION	8. Exalted feeling arising from a sense of triumph, power or relief
OBDURATE	9. Intractable; not giving in
DAUNTLESS	10. Fearless; bold
EXASPERATION	11. The state of extremely annoyed or irritated
PRODIGIOUS	12. Enormous, extraordinary; marvelous
HEEDLESS	13. Paying little or no attention; unmindful
SMITTEN	14. Afflicted
AUDACIOUS	15. Arrogantly insolent
DESPONDENT	16. Feeling disheartened or dejected
MOROSE	17. Melancholy; gloomy; ill-humored
AGUE	18. A recurrent chill or fit of shivering
CONDESCENSION	19. The act of coming down voluntarily to the level of inferiors
IMPRECATIONS	20. Curses

Red Badge of Courage Vocabulary Fill In The Blanks 4

1. Rest
2. An open condemnation or censure
3. Acting with little interest or care
4. Detected; perceived
5. Heating or noisy quarrel
6. Wretched; of the most contemptible kind
7. Humorous and flippant; playfully jocular
8. Fearless; bold
9. Made wet and limp
10. Portentous; foreboding
11. Lacking self-composure
12. Confidence; dependence; trust
13. Caused to do something
14. Afflicted
15. Eyes
16. Morose, sulky
17. A curse or slander
18. The condition of being unknown
19. Endless
20. The act of coming down voluntarily to the level of inferiors

Red Badge of Courage Vocabulary Fill In The Blanks 4 Answer Key

REPOSE	1. Rest
DENUNCIATION	2. An open condemnation or censure
PERFUNCTORY	3. Acting with little interest or care
DISCERNED	4. Detected; perceived
ALTERCATION	5. Heating or noisy quarrel
ABJECT	6. Wretched; of the most contemptible kind
FACETIOUS	7. Humorous and flippant; playfully jocular
DAUNTLESS	8. Fearless; bold
BEDRAGGLED	9. Made wet and limp
OMINOUS	10. Portentous; foreboding
DISCONCERTED	11. Lacking self-composure
RELIANCE	12. Confidence; dependence; trust
OBLIGED	13. Caused to do something
SMITTEN	14. Afflicted
ORBS	15. Eyes
SULLEN	16. Morose, sulky
MALEDICTION	17. A curse or slander
OBSCURITY	18. The condition of being unknown
INTERMINABLE	19. Endless
CONDESCENSION	20. The act of coming down voluntarily to the level of inferiors

Red Badge of Courage Vocabulary Matching 1

___ 1. IMPRECATIONS A. The condition of being unknown
___ 2. PLACIDLY B. Melancholy; gloomy; ill-humored
___ 3. VINDICATION C. Massive
___ 4. FACETIOUS D. Detected; perceived
___ 5. BEDRAGGLED E. Humorous and flippant; playfully jocular
___ 6. AUDACIOUS F. Arrogantly insolent
___ 7. OMINOUS G. Portentous; foreboding
___ 8. REPOSE H. Confidence; dependence; trust
___ 9. SULLEN I. Lacking self-composure
___ 10. BLITHE J. Outwardly calm or composed; complacent
___ 11. DESPONDENT K. Eyes
___ 12. SMITTEN L. Afflicted
___ 13. DISCONCERTED M. Morose, sulky
___ 14. SINUOUS N. Feeling disheartened or dejected
___ 15. ORBS O. A recurrent chill or fit of shivering
___ 16. SARDONIC P. Cheerful; casual; carefree
___ 17. OBDURATE Q. Curses
___ 18. MOROSE R. Intractable; not giving in
___ 19. INDIGNANTLY S. Rest
___ 20. RELIANCE T. With an anger aroused by something unjust
___ 21. OBSCURITY U. Temporary mental confusion
___ 22. DELIRIUM V. Winding
___ 23. AGUE W. Made wet and limp
___ 24. PONDEROUS X. The evidence or argument that justifies an act
___ 25. DISCERNED Y. Mocking; cynical

Red Badge of Courage Vocabulary Matching 1 Answer Key

Q - 1.	IMPRECATIONS	A.	The condition of being unknown
J - 2.	PLACIDLY	B.	Melancholy; gloomy; ill-humored
X - 3.	VINDICATION	C.	Massive
E - 4.	FACETIOUS	D.	Detected; perceived
W - 5.	BEDRAGGLED	E.	Humorous and flippant; playfully jocular
F - 6.	AUDACIOUS	F.	Arrogantly insolent
G - 7.	OMINOUS	G.	Portentous; foreboding
S - 8.	REPOSE	H.	Confidence; dependence; trust
M - 9.	SULLEN	I.	Lacking self-composure
P - 10.	BLITHE	J.	Outwardly calm or composed; complacent
N - 11.	DESPONDENT	K.	Eyes
L - 12.	SMITTEN	L.	Afflicted
I - 13.	DISCONCERTED	M.	Morose, sulky
V - 14.	SINUOUS	N.	Feeling disheartened or dejected
K - 15.	ORBS	O.	A recurrent chill or fit of shivering
Y - 16.	SARDONIC	P.	Cheerful; casual; carefree
R - 17.	OBDURATE	Q.	Curses
B - 18.	MOROSE	R.	Intractable; not giving in
T - 19.	INDIGNANTLY	S.	Rest
H - 20.	RELIANCE	T.	With an anger aroused by something unjust
A - 21.	OBSCURITY	U.	Temporary mental confusion
U - 22.	DELIRIUM	V.	Winding
O - 23.	AGUE	W.	Made wet and limp
C - 24.	PONDEROUS	X.	The evidence or argument that justifies an act
D - 25.	DISCERNED	Y.	Mocking; cynical

Red Badge of Courage Vocabulary Matching 2

___ 1. SPECTER
___ 2. BLITHE
___ 3. ABJECT
___ 4. ALTERCATION
___ 5. OBSCURITY
___ 6. FACETIOUS
___ 7. MALEDICTION
___ 8. RELIANCE
___ 9. ORBS
___ 10. MOROSE
___ 11. DESPONDENT
___ 12. BEDRAGGLED
___ 13. PONDEROUS
___ 14. DISCONCERTED
___ 15. AGUE
___ 16. HEEDLESS
___ 17. OMINOUS
___ 18. IMPENDING
___ 19. EXASPERATION
___ 20. OBDURATE
___ 21. DENOTED
___ 22. IMPRECATIONS
___ 23. SULLEN
___ 24. REPROOF
___ 25. INTERMINABLE

A. Humorous and flippant; playfully jocular
B. Feeling disheartened or dejected
C. Eyes
D. Morose, sulky
E. Ghost; phantasm
F. A recurrent chill or fit of shivering
G. Endless
H. Cheerful; casual; carefree
I. Paying little or no attention; unmindful
J. Wretched; of the most contemptible kind
K. The state of extremely annoyed or irritated
L. The condition of being unknown
M. Made wet and limp
N. Likely to happen soon
O. Melancholy; gloomy; ill-humored
P. A curse or slander
Q. Portentous; foreboding
R. Lacking self-composure
S. Confidence; dependence; trust
T. Curses
U. Reprimand
V. Marked; indicated; signified
W. Intractable; not giving in
X. Heating or noisy quarrel
Y. Massive

Red Badge of Courage Vocabulary Matching 2 Answer Key

E - 1. SPECTER	A.	Humorous and flippant; playfully jocular
H - 2. BLITHE	B.	Feeling disheartened or dejected
J - 3. ABJECT	C.	Eyes
X - 4. ALTERCATION	D.	Morose, sulky
L - 5. OBSCURITY	E.	Ghost; phantasm
A - 6. FACETIOUS	F.	A recurrent chill or fit of shivering
P - 7. MALEDICTION	G.	Endless
S - 8. RELIANCE	H.	Cheerful; casual; carefree
C - 9. ORBS	I.	Paying little or no attention; unmindful
O -10. MOROSE	J.	Wretched; of the most contemptible kind
B -11. DESPONDENT	K.	The state of extremely annoyed or irritated
M -12. BEDRAGGLED	L.	The condition of being unknown
Y -13. PONDEROUS	M.	Made wet and limp
R -14. DISCONCERTED	N.	Likely to happen soon
F -15. AGUE	O.	Melancholy; gloomy; ill-humored
I -16. HEEDLESS	P.	A curse or slander
Q -17. OMINOUS	Q.	Portentous; foreboding
N -18. IMPENDING	R.	Lacking self-composure
K -19. EXASPERATION	S.	Confidence; dependence; trust
W -20. OBDURATE	T.	Curses
V -21. DENOTED	U.	Reprimand
T -22. IMPRECATIONS	V.	Marked; indicated; signified
D -23. SULLEN	W.	Intractable; not giving in
U -24. REPROOF	X.	Heating or noisy quarrel
G -25. INTERMINABLE	Y.	Massive

Copyrighted

Red Badge of Courage Vocabulary Matching 3

___ 1. SMITTEN   A. Arrogantly insolent
___ 2. LUDICROUS   B. Caused to do something
___ 3. OBLIGED   C. Made wet and limp
___ 4. ALTERCATION   D. The condition of being unknown
___ 5. OBSCURITY   E. Humorous and flippant; playfully jocular
___ 6. REPROOF   F. Heating or noisy quarrel
___ 7. CONDESCENSION   G. With an anger aroused by something unjust
___ 8. DELIRIUM   H. A curse or slander
___ 9. DESPONDENT   I. Likely to happen soon
___ 10. ANNIHILATED   J. Laughable because of obvious absurdity or incongruity
___ 11. VANQUISHED   K. Feeling disheartened or dejected
___ 12. AUDACIOUS   L. Wiped out; destroyed completely
___ 13. INTERMINABLE   M. Defeated; overcome
___ 14. MALEDICTION   N. Melancholy; gloomy; ill-humored
___ 15. DISCONCERTED   O. Endless
___ 16. INDIGNANTLY   P. Reprimand
___ 17. DENUNCIATION   Q. An open condemnation or censure
___ 18. AGUE   R. Temporary mental confusion
___ 19. OBDURATE   S. A recurrent chill or fit of shivering
___ 20. IMPENDING   T. Afflicted
___ 21. FACETIOUS   U. Intractable; not giving in
___ 22. PERFUNCTORY   V. Lacking self-composure
___ 23. MOROSE   W. The act of coming down voluntarily to the level of inferiors
___ 24. PROXIMITY   X. Acting with little interest or care
___ 25. BEDRAGGLED   Y. Closeness

Red Badge of Courage Vocabulary Matching 3 Answer Key

T - 1. SMITTEN
J - 2. LUDICROUS
B - 3. OBLIGED
F - 4. ALTERCATION
D - 5. OBSCURITY
P - 6. REPROOF
W - 7. CONDESCENSION
R - 8. DELIRIUM
K - 9. DESPONDENT
L - 10. ANNIHILATED
M - 11. VANQUISHED
A - 12. AUDACIOUS
O - 13. INTERMINABLE
H - 14. MALEDICTION
V - 15. DISCONCERTED
G - 16. INDIGNANTLY
Q - 17. DENUNCIATION
S - 18. AGUE
U - 19. OBDURATE
I - 20. IMPENDING
E - 21. FACETIOUS
X - 22. PERFUNCTORY
N - 23. MOROSE
Y - 24. PROXIMITY
C - 25. BEDRAGGLED

A. Arrogantly insolent
B. Caused to do something
C. Made wet and limp
D. The condition of being unknown
E. Humorous and flippant; playfully jocular
F. Heating or noisy quarrel
G. With an anger aroused by something unjust
H. A curse or slander
I. Likely to happen soon
J. Laughable because of obvious absurdity or incongruity
K. Feeling disheartened or dejected
L. Wiped out; destroyed completely
M. Defeated; overcome
N. Melancholy; gloomy; ill-humored
O. Endless
P. Reprimand
Q. An open condemnation or censure
R. Temporary mental confusion
S. A recurrent chill or fit of shivering
T. Afflicted
U. Intractable; not giving in
V. Lacking self-composure
W. The act of coming down voluntarily to the level of inferiors
X. Acting with little interest or care
Y. Closeness

Red Badge of Courage Vocabulary Matching 4

___ 1. REPROOF
___ 2. ORBS
___ 3. CONDESCENSION
___ 4. ABJECT
___ 5. AUDACIOUS
___ 6. PONDEROUS
___ 7. MOROSE
___ 8. IMPENDING
___ 9. ANNIHILATED
___10. BLITHE
___11. PRODIGIOUS
___12. SULLEN
___13. OBSCURITY
___14. DENUNCIATION
___15. ELATION
___16. DELIRIUM
___17. AGUE
___18. REPOSE
___19. IMPETUS
___20. RELIANCE
___21. LUDICROUS
___22. OBLIGED
___23. MALEDICTION
___24. INDIGNANTLY
___25. VINDICATION

A. Likely to happen soon
B. Eyes
C. Wiped out; destroyed completely
D. A recurrent chill or fit of shivering
E. The condition of being unknown
F. Cheerful; casual; carefree
G. Wretched; of the most contemptible kind
H. An open condemnation or censure
I. Exalted feeling arising from a sense of triumph, power or relief
J. With an anger aroused by something unjust
K. Massive
L. Laughable because of obvious absurdity or incongruity
M. A curse or slander
N. Arrogantly insolent
O. Morose, sulky
P. Temporary mental confusion
Q. Reprimand
R. Melancholy; gloomy; ill-humored
S. Enormous, extraordinary; marvelous
T. The evidence or argument that justifies an act
U. Rest
V. Impelling force; impulse; stimulus
W. The act of coming down voluntarily to the level of inferiors
X. Caused to do something
Y. Confidence; dependence; trust

Red Badge of Courage Vocabulary Matching 4 Answer Key

Q - 1. REPROOF		A. Likely to happen soon
B - 2. ORBS		B. Eyes
W - 3. CONDESCENSION		C. Wiped out; destroyed completely
G - 4. ABJECT		D. A recurrent chill or fit of shivering
N - 5. AUDACIOUS		E. The condition of being unknown
K - 6. PONDEROUS		F. Cheerful; casual; carefree
R - 7. MOROSE		G. Wretched; of the most contemptible kind
A - 8. IMPENDING		H. An open condemnation or censure
C - 9. ANNIHILATED		I. Exalted feeling arising from a sense of triumph, power or relief
F - 10. BLITHE		J. With an anger aroused by something unjust
S - 11. PRODIGIOUS		K. Massive
O - 12. SULLEN		L. Laughable because of obvious absurdity or incongruity
E - 13. OBSCURITY		M. A curse or slander
H - 14. DENUNCIATION		N. Arrogantly insolent
I - 15. ELATION		O. Morose, sulky
P - 16. DELIRIUM		P. Temporary mental confusion
D - 17. AGUE		Q. Reprimand
U - 18. REPOSE		R. Melancholy; gloomy; ill-humored
V - 19. IMPETUS		S. Enormous, extraordinary; marvelous
Y - 20. RELIANCE		T. The evidence or argument that justifies an act
L - 21. LUDICROUS		U. Rest
X - 22. OBLIGED		V. Impelling force; impulse; stimulus
M - 23. MALEDICTION		W. The act of coming down voluntarily to the level of inferiors
J - 24. INDIGNANTLY		X. Caused to do something
T - 25. VINDICATION		Y. Confidence; dependence; trust

Red Badge of Courage Vocabulary Magic Squares 1

Match the definition with the vocabulary word. Put your answers in the magic squares below. When your answers are correct, all columns and rows will add to the same number.

A. PRODIGIOUS
B. DENOTED
C. CONDESCENSION
D. VANQUISHED
E. SMITTEN
F. AUDACIOUS
G. REPOSE
H. INDIGNANTLY
I. HEEDLESS
J. PONDEROUS
K. INTERMINABLE
L. MALEDICTION
M. REPROOF
N. DISCERNED
O. OMINOUS
P. IMPETUS

1. Enormous, extraordinary; marvelous
2. Detected; perceived
3. Massive
4. Afflicted
5. Rest
6. A curse or slander
7. Impelling force; impulse; stimulus
8. The act of coming down voluntarily to the level of inferiors
9. Portentous; foreboding
10. Defeated; overcome
11. With an anger aroused by something unjust
12. Endless
13. Paying little or no attention; unmindful
14. Arrogantly insolent
15. Marked; indicated; signified
16. Reprimand

A=	B=	C=	D=
E=	F=	G=	H=
I=	J=	K=	L=
M=	N=	O=	P=

Red Badge of Courage Vocabulary Magic Squares 1 Answer Key

Match the definition with the vocabulary word. Put your answers in the magic squares below. When your answers are correct, all columns and rows will add to the same number.

A. PRODIGIOUS
B. DENOTED
C. CONDESCENSION
D. VANQUISHED
E. SMITTEN
F. AUDACIOUS
G. REPOSE
H. INDIGNANTLY
I. HEEDLESS
J. PONDEROUS
K. INTERMINABLE
L. MALEDICTION
M. REPROOF
N. DISCERNED
O. OMINOUS
P. IMPETUS

1. Enormous, extraordinary; marvelous
2. Detected; perceived
3. Massive
4. Afflicted
5. Rest
6. A curse or slander
7. Impelling force; impulse; stimulus
8. The act of coming down voluntarily to the level of inferiors
9. Portentous; foreboding
10. Defeated; overcome
11. With an anger aroused by something unjust
12. Endless
13. Paying little or no attention; unmindful
14. Arrogantly insolent
15. Marked; indicated; signified
16. Reprimand

A=1	B=15	C=8	D=10
E=4	F=14	G=5	H=11
I=13	J=3	K=12	L=6
M=16	N=2	O=9	P=7

Red Badge of Courage Vocabulary Magic Squares 2

Match the definition with the vocabulary word. Put your answers in the magic squares below. When your answers are correct, all columns and rows will add to the same number.

A. ORBS
B. IMPENDING
C. PLACIDLY
D. FORMIDABLE
E. EXASPERATION
F. PRODIGIOUS
G. BEDRAGGLED
H. SMITTEN
I. REPROOF
J. ABJECT
K. FACETIOUS
L. VINDICATION
M. DENOTED
N. PERFUNCTORY
O. INTERMINABLE
P. SPECTER

1. Outwardly calm or composed; complacent
2. Wretched; of the most contemptible kind
3. Enormous, extraordinary; marvelous
4. Endless
5. Ghost; phantasm
6. The state of extremely annoyed or irritated
7. Reprimand
8. Arousing fear or dread; awesome; difficult to overtake
9. Marked; indicated; signified
10. Afflicted
11. The evidence or argument that justifies an act
12. Eyes
13. Likely to happen soon
14. Humorous and flippant; playfully jocular
15. Made wet and limp
16. Acting with little interest or care

A=	B=	C=	D=
E=	F=	G=	H=
I=	J=	K=	L=
M=	N=	O=	P=

Red Badge of Courage Vocabulary Magic Squares 2 Answer Key

Match the definition with the vocabulary word. Put your answers in the magic squares below. When your answers are correct, all columns and rows will add to the same number.

A. ORBS
B. IMPENDING
C. PLACIDLY
D. FORMIDABLE
E. EXASPERATION
F. PRODIGIOUS
G. BEDRAGGLED
H. SMITTEN
I. REPROOF
J. ABJECT
K. FACETIOUS
L. VINDICATION
M. DENOTED
N. PERFUNCTORY
O. INTERMINABLE
P. SPECTER

1. Outwardly calm or composed; complacent
2. Wretched; of the most contemptible kind
3. Enormous, extraordinary; marvelous
4. Endless
5. Ghost; phantasm
6. The state of extremely annoyed or irritated
7. Reprimand
8. Arousing fear or dread; awesome; difficult to overtake
9. Marked; indicated; signified
10. Afflicted
11. The evidence or argument that justifies an act
12. Eyes
13. Likely to happen soon
14. Humorous and flippant; playfully jocular
15. Made wet and limp
16. Acting with little interest or care

A=12	B=13	C=1	D=8
E=6	F=3	G=15	H=10
I=7	J=2	K=14	L=11
M=9	N=16	O=4	P=5

Red Badge of Courage Vocabulary Magic Squares 3

Match the definition with the vocabulary word. Put your answers in the magic squares below. When your answers are correct, all columns and rows will add to the same number.

A. ELATION
B. VANQUISHED
C. FORMIDABLE
D. BLITHE
E. MALEDICTION
F. INTERMINABLE
G. REPOSE
H. BEDRAGGLED
I. FACETIOUS
J. CHAOS
K. HEEDLESS
L. OMINOUS
M. DISCONCERTED
N. AGUE
O. AUDACIOUS
P. ALTERCATION

1. Arrogantly insolent
2. Cheerful; casual; carefree
3. Total disorder or confusion
4. A curse or slander
5. Humorous and flippant; playfully jocular
6. Endless
7. Heating or noisy quarrel
8. Arousing fear or dread; awesome; difficult to overtake
9. Made wet and limp
10. Paying little or no attention; unmindful
11. Exalted feeling arising from a sense of triumph, power or relief
12. A recurrent chill or fit of shivering
13. Defeated; overcome
14. Lacking self-composure
15. Rest
16. Portentous; foreboding

A=	B=	C=	D=
E=	F=	G=	H=
I=	J=	K=	L=
M=	N=	O=	P=

Red Badge of Courage Vocabulary Magic Squares 3 Answer Key

Match the definition with the vocabulary word. Put your answers in the magic squares below. When your answers are correct, all columns and rows will add to the same number.

A. ELATION
B. VANQUISHED
C. FORMIDABLE
D. BLITHE
E. MALEDICTION
F. INTERMINABLE
G. REPOSE
H. BEDRAGGLED
I. FACETIOUS
J. CHAOS
K. HEEDLESS
L. OMINOUS
M. DISCONCERTED
N. AGUE
O. AUDACIOUS
P. ALTERCATION

1. Arrogantly insolent
2. Cheerful; casual; carefree
3. Total disorder or confusion
4. A curse or slander
5. Humorous and flippant; playfully jocular
6. Endless
7. Heating or noisy quarrel
8. Arousing fear or dread; awesome; difficult to overtake
9. Made wet and limp
10. Paying little or no attention; unmindful
11. Exalted feeling arising from a sense of triumph, power or relief
12. A recurrent chill or fit of shivering
13. Defeated; overcome
14. Lacking self-composure
15. Rest
16. Portentous; foreboding

A=11	B=13	C=8	D=2
E=4	F=6	G=15	H=9
I=5	J=3	K=10	L=16
M=14	N=12	O=1	P=7

Red Badge of Courage Vocabulary Magic Squares 4

Match the definition with the vocabulary word. Put your answers in the magic squares below. When your answers are correct, all columns and rows will add to the same number.

A. ALTERCATION
B. PLACIDLY
C. DISCERNED
D. SPECTER
E. OMINOUS
F. SARDONIC
G. IMPETUS
H. IMPRECATIONS
I. AGUE
J. LUDICROUS
K. MOROSE
L. REPROOF
M. SULLEN
N. OBSCURITY
O. RELIANCE
P. INDIGNANTLY

1. Curses
2. Morose, sulky
3. Outwardly calm or composed; complacent
4. Melancholy; gloomy; ill-humored
5. Laughable because of obvious absurdity or incongruity
6. Detected; perceived
7. With an anger aroused by something unjust
8. Portentous; foreboding
9. Confidence; dependence; trust
10. Mocking; cynical
11. A recurrent chill or fit of shivering
12. Ghost; phantasm
13. Heating or noisy quarrel
14. Reprimand
15. Impelling force; impulse; stimulus
16. The condition of being unknown

A=	B=	C=	D=
E=	F=	G=	H=
I=	J=	K=	L=
M=	N=	O=	P=

Red Badge of Courage Vocabulary Magic Squares 4 Answer Key

Match the definition with the vocabulary word. Put your answers in the magic squares below. When your answers are correct, all columns and rows will add to the same number.

A. ALTERCATION
B. PLACIDLY
C. DISCERNED
D. SPECTER
E. OMINOUS
F. SARDONIC
G. IMPETUS
H. IMPRECATIONS
I. AGUE
J. LUDICROUS
K. MOROSE
L. REPROOF
M. SULLEN
N. OBSCURITY
O. RELIANCE
P. INDIGNANTLY

1. Curses
2. Morose, sulky
3. Outwardly calm or composed; complacent
4. Melancholy; gloomy; ill-humored
5. Laughable because of obvious absurdity or incongruity
6. Detected; perceived
7. With an anger aroused by something unjust
8. Portentous; foreboding
9. Confidence; dependence; trust
10. Mocking; cynical
11. A recurrent chill or fit of shivering
12. Ghost; phantasm
13. Heating or noisy quarrel
14. Reprimand
15. Impelling force; impulse; stimulus
16. The condition of being unknown

A=13	B=3	C=6	D=12
E=8	F=10	G=15	H=1
I=11	J=5	K=4	L=14
M=2	N=16	O=9	P=7

Red Badge of Courage Vocabulary Word Search 1

Words are placed backwards, forward, diagonally, up and down. Clues listed below can help you find the words. Circle the hidden vocabulary words in the maze.

```
S  S  E  L  D  E  E  H  D  E  L  I  R  I  U  M  V  O  P
U  M  J  X  F  K  D  L  W  N  B  X  F  M  O  P  A  B  R
O  P  T  H  G  Q  M  U  C  B  P  L  Z  L  B  O  N  S  O
I  R  V  S  F  Y  G  D  L  F  S  M  S  W  L  N  Q  C  D
C  M  A  N  N  I  H  I  L  A  T  E  D  G  I  D  U  U  I
A  B  P  N  Q  K  T  C  P  P  C  P  V  G  G  E  I  R  G
D  Y  N  R  B  H  D  R  R  T  H  S  L  E  E  R  S  I  I
U  D  Q  T  E  V  D  O  O  K  O  D  L  X  D  O  H  T  O
A  A  B  J  E  C  T  U  X  C  C  B  X  R  D  U  E  Y  U
E  U  O  P  V  R  A  S  I  K  A  X  D  M  E  S  D  H  S
L  N  M  P  G  T  Y  T  M  N  O  Q  O  U  N  P  T  G  J
A  T  I  D  E  C  N  A  I  L  E  R  E  P  R  O  O  F  P
T  L  N  I  Z  Z  Q  M  T  O  O  M  B  R  E  A  F  S  J
I  E  O  S  V  G  R  W  Y  S  N  I  S  S  C  P  T  N  E
O  S  U  C  S  E  R  H  E  D  M  S  Y  J  S  F  X  E  P
N  S  S  O  T  E  X  A  S  P  E  R  A  T  I  O  N  L  R
C  K  A  N  X  Y  S  C  E  P  L  N  T  R  D  V  Q  L  E
X  H  I  C  Y  J  J  T  N  W  E  A  O  C  D  P  N  U  L
C  T  W  E  M  K  U  F  B  Z  N  C  C  T  Y  O  G  S  S
N  N  N  R  K  S  I  N  U  O  U  S  T  I  E  A  N  P  T
L  R  Q  T  F  A  C  E  T  I  O  U  S  E  D  D  K  I  T
Z  G  D  E  N  U  N  C  I  A  T  I  O  N  R  L  M  X  C
V  I  N  D  I  C  A  T  I  O  N  C  P  S  M  K  Y  B  Q
```

A recurrent chill or fit of shivering (4)
An open condemnation or censure (12)
Arrogantly insolent (9)
Caused to do something (7)
Cheerful; casual; carefree (6)
Closeness (9)
Confidence; dependence; trust (8)
Curses (12)
Defeated; overcome (10)
Detected; perceived (9)
Endless (12)
Enormous, extraordinary; marvelous (10)
Exalted feeling arising from a sense of triumph, power or relief (7)
Eyes (4)
Fearless; bold (9)
Ghost; phantasm (7)
Humorous and flippant; playfully jocular (9)
Impelling force; impulse; stimulus (7)
Intractable; not giving in (8)
Lacking self-composure (12)
Laughable because of obvious absurdity or incongruity (9)
Marked; indicated; signified (7)
Massive (9)
Melancholy; gloomy; ill-humored (6)
Mocking; cynical (8)
Morose, sulky (6)
Outwardly calm or composed; complacent (8)
Paying little or no attention; unmindful (8)
Portentous; foreboding (7)
Reprimand (7)
Rest (6)
Temporary mental confusion (8)
The condition of being unknown (9)
The evidence or argument that justifies an act (11)
The state of extremely annoyed or irritated (12)
Total disorder or confusion (5)
Winding (7)
Wiped out; destroyed completely (11)
Wretched; of the most contemptible kind (6)

Red Badge of Courage Vocabulary Word Search 1 Answer Key

Words are placed backwards, forward, diagonally, up and down. Clues listed below can help you find the words. Circle the hidden vocabulary words in the maze.

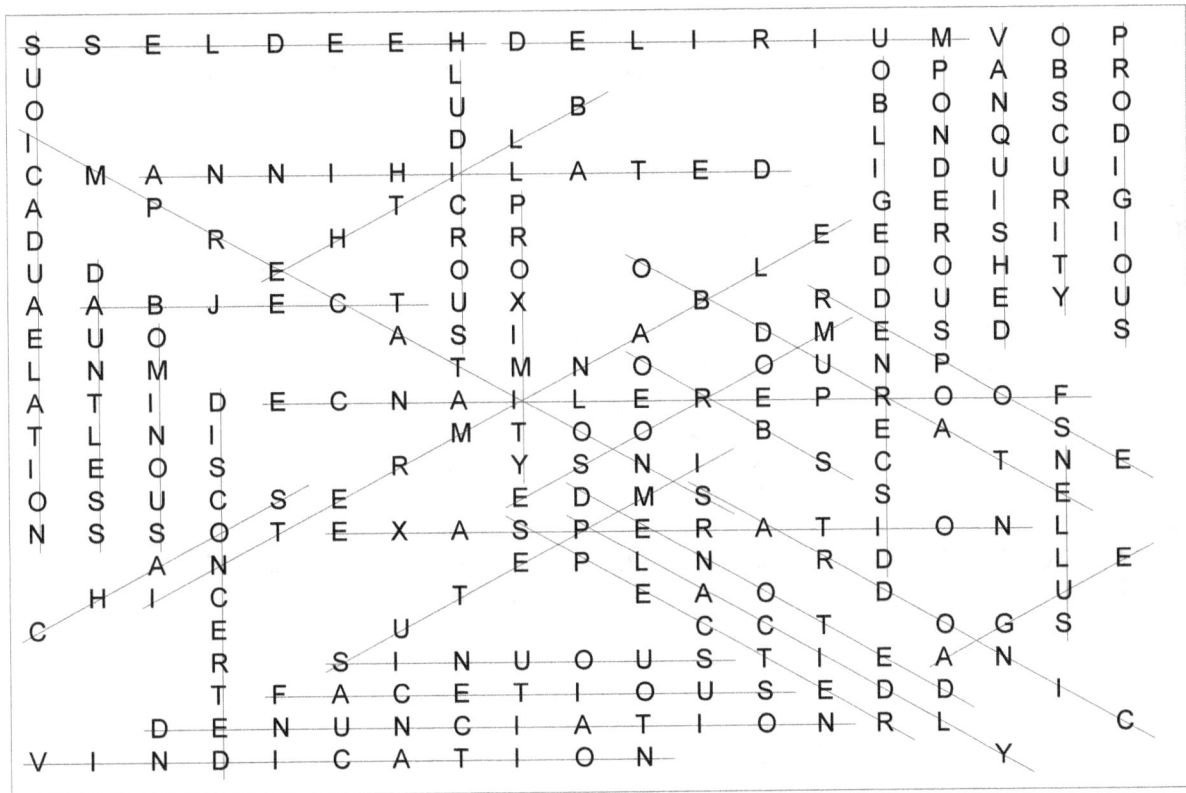

A recurrent chill or fit of shivering (4)
An open condemnation or censure (12)
Arrogantly insolent (9)
Caused to do something (7)
Cheerful; casual; carefree (6)
Closeness (9)
Confidence; dependence; trust (8)
Curses (12)
Defeated; overcome (10)
Detected; perceived (9)
Endless (12)
Enormous, extraordinary; marvelous (10)
Exalted feeling arising from a sense of triumph, power or relief (7)
Eyes (4)
Fearless; bold (9)
Ghost; phantasm (7)
Humorous and flippant; playfully jocular (9)
Impelling force; impulse; stimulus (7)
Intractable; not giving in (8)
Lacking self-composure (12)
Laughable because of obvious absurdity or incongruity (9)
Marked; indicated; signified (7)
Massive (9)
Melancholy; gloomy; ill-humored (6)
Mocking; cynical (8)
Morose, sulky (6)
Outwardly calm or composed; complacent (8)
Paying little or no attention; unmindful (8)
Portentous; foreboding (7)
Reprimand (7)
Rest (6)
Temporary mental confusion (8)
The condition of being unknown (9)
The evidence or argument that justifies an act (11)
The state of extremely annoyed or irritated (12)
Total disorder or confusion (5)
Winding (7)
Wiped out; destroyed completely (11)
Wretched; of the most contemptible kind (6)

Red Badge of Courage Vocabulary Word Search 2

Words are placed backwards, forward, diagonally, up and down. Clues listed below can help you find the words. Circle the hidden vocabulary words in the maze.

```
S I N U O U S E X A S P E R A T I O N
S M G W H M D D T H E E D L E S S H Y
B F I E L Y I F O R M I D A B L E L R
S H R T D V I N D I C A T I O N T L Z
D V E A T R S U O I T E C A F N H P L
E R P R D E H S I Q N A V A S O L X
T C O U B M N J F M S S Y N U N S A Y
A N S D C A N H C Q N L G O D Q A C M
L L E B P L R T B O C I I E R J R I T
I H T O R E G V I C D C R J L C D D T
H P J E R D R T M N A O B P H Q O L C
I S H E R I A F I D U M L A Y W N Y H
N L U D I C R O U S P R O X I M I T Y
N G B J E T A A R N J S D R S P C I L
A S J R F I T T P E C C D O E T M C
X C P C Z O E T I Y L T Y Y J S X P M
K M R E B N J L S O N I O B S C E E V
I Q F P C F Q H A R N B A R B Q T N T
K G N L Z T B M Z T T J Z N Y G E D Z
M U I R I L E D B L I T H E C L V I L
O B L I G E D R K B C O C K L E G N Z
L P R O D I G I O U S V N U G J J G T
D E N O T E D O R B S H S U T E P M I
```

A curse or slander (11)
A recurrent chill or fit of shivering (4)
Acting with little interest or care (11)
Afflicted (7)
Arousing fear or dread; awesome; difficult to overtake (10)
Arrogantly insolent (9)
Caused to do something (7)
Cheerful; casual; carefree (6)
Closeness (9)
Confidence; dependence; trust (8)
Curses (12)
Defeated; overcome (10)
Enormous, extraordinary; marvelous (10)
Exalted feeling arising from a sense of triumph, power or relief (7)
Eyes (4)
Ghost; phantasm (7)
Heating or noisy quarrel (11)
Humorous and flippant; playfully jocular (9)
Impelling force; impulse; stimulus (7)
Intractable; not giving in (8)

Laughable because of obvious absurdity or incongruity (9)
Likely to happen soon (9)
Marked; indicated; signified (7)
Massive (9)
Melancholy; gloomy; ill-humored (6)
Mocking; cynical (8)
Morose, sulky (6)
Outwardly calm or composed; complacent (8)
Paying little or no attention; unmindful (8)
Portentous; foreboding (7)
Rest (6)
Temporary mental confusion (8)
The evidence or argument that justifies an act (11)
The state of extremely annoyed or irritated (12)
Total disorder or confusion (5)
Winding (7)
Wiped out; destroyed completely (11)
With an anger aroused by something unjust (11)
Wretched; of the most contemptible kind (6)

Red Badge of Courage Vocabulary Word Search 2 Answer Key

Words are placed backwards, forward, diagonally, up and down. Clues listed below can help you find the words. Circle the hidden vocabulary words in the maze.

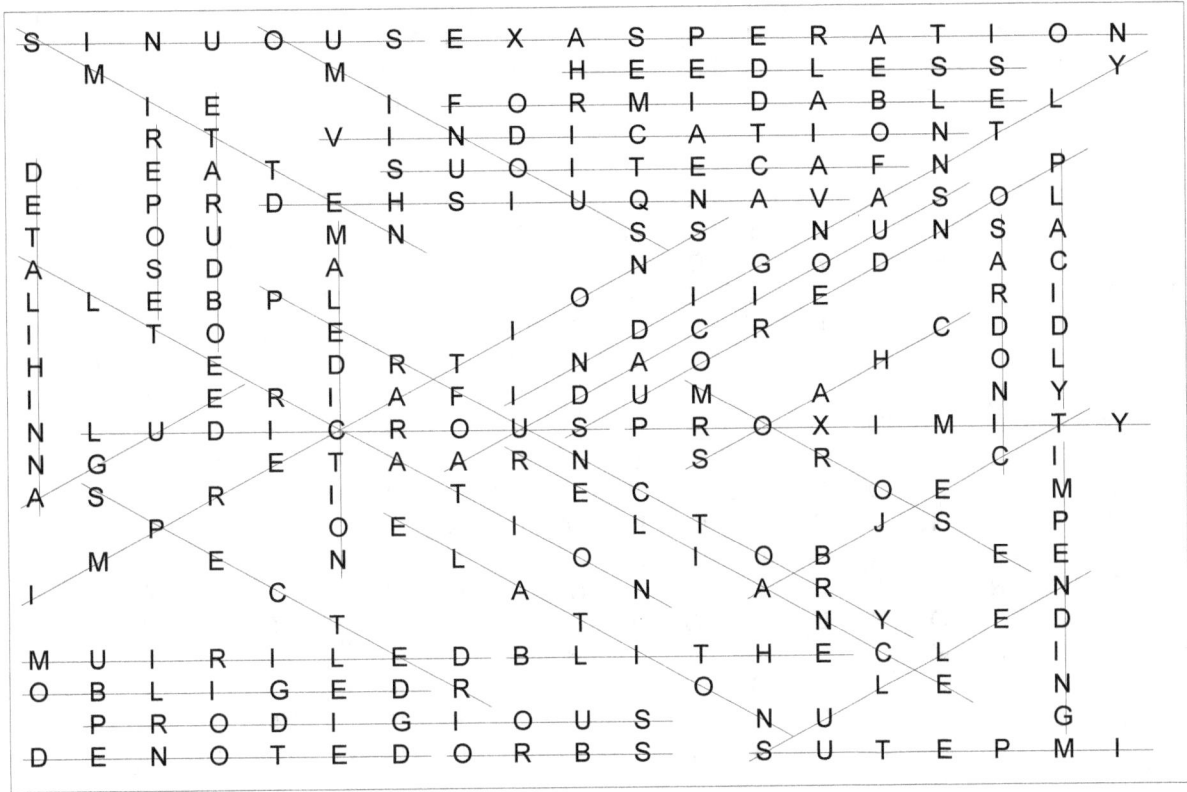

A curse or slander (11)
A recurrent chill or fit of shivering (4)
Acting with little interest or care (11)
Afflicted (7)
Arousing fear or dread; awesome; difficult to overtake (10)
Arrogantly insolent (9)
Caused to do something (7)
Cheerful; casual; carefree (6)
Closeness (9)
Confidence; dependence; trust (8)
Curses (12)
Defeated; overcome (10)
Enormous, extraordinary; marvelous (10)
Exalted feeling arising from a sense of triumph, power or relief (7)
Eyes (4)
Ghost; phantasm (7)
Heating or noisy quarrel (11)
Humorous and flippant; playfully jocular (9)
Impelling force; impulse; stimulus (7)
Intractable; not giving in (8)

Laughable because of obvious absurdity or incongruity (9)
Likely to happen soon (9)
Marked; indicated; signified (7)
Massive (9)
Melancholy; gloomy; ill-humored (6)
Mocking; cynical (8)
Morose, sulky (6)
Outwardly calm or composed; complacent (8)
Paying little or no attention; unmindful (8)
Portentous; foreboding (7)
Rest (6)
Temporary mental confusion (8)
The evidence or argument that justifies an act (11)
The state of extremely annoyed or irritated (12)
Total disorder or confusion (5)
Winding (7)
Wiped out; destroyed completely (11)
With an anger aroused by something unjust (11)
Wretched; of the most contemptible kind (6)

Red Badge of Courage Vocabulary Word Search 3

Words are placed backwards, forward, diagonally, up and down. Words listed below are included in the maze. Circle the hidden vocabulary words in the maze.

```
F A C E T I O U S T T S B N P P A R L
H V L T P S R M R Q S X L O R E D D U
S V K A V C B Q E E C D I I O R D S D
T Z Q R Z X T L L U J I T D F A J I
L Z F U W Y A D I G M S H A I U C P C
I T Q D K T E D A A J C E I G N I L R
H M J B I E D B N M A E R C I C O A O
Z P P O H T E K C H L R K N O T U C U
S D N E X B L N E B T N J U U O S I S
W P B D N X I B A F E E B N S R F D N
G N E N Z D R N S S R D Y E F Y N L O
C H K C N O I S N E C S E D N O C Y I
H W B F T M U N M H A F E D N K L S T
A S V Z R E M C G Y T G E Z L T O U A
O D M E S O R O M V I T D P N S B L C
S M T I N W S S Q L O Q O A U S S L R
N N I S T D Q L B N N N T F E C E E P
I R R N I T R O E J D G E O A L L N M
P Y E J O N E D W E I P O S B T R M M
W D P L M U N R D M R B F J N I K I
L H O N P R S O N I P R L H E U T M C
T J S X M Z U I U E O B S R C A Y S Y
W Z E G C S J B R S V F H Q T D K X B
```

ABJECT	FACETIOUS	ORBS
AGUE	HEEDLESS	PERFUNCTORY
ALTERCATION	IMPENDING	PLACIDLY
AUDACIOUS	IMPETUS	PONDEROUS
BLITHE	IMPRECATIONS	PRODIGIOUS
CHAOS	INDIGNANTLY	RELIANCE
CONDESCENSION	INTERMINABLE	REPOSE
DAUNTLESS	LUDICROUS	REPROOF
DELIRIUM	MOROSE	SINUOUS
DENOTED	OBDURATE	SMITTEN
DENUNCIATION	OBLIGED	SPECTER
DISCERNED	OBSCURITY	SULLEN
ELATION	OMINOUS	

Red Badge of Courage Vocabulary Word Search 3 Answer Key

Words are placed backwards, forward, diagonally, up and down. Words listed below are included in the maze. Circle the hidden vocabulary words in the maze.

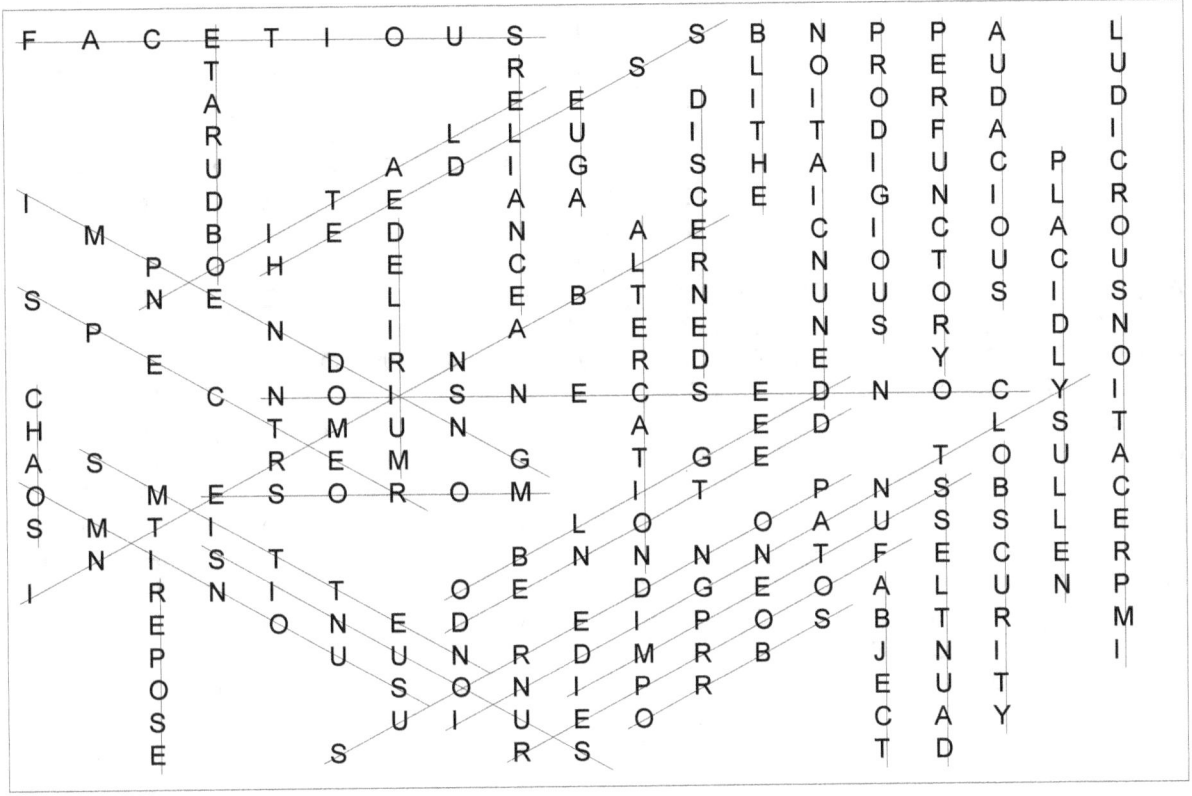

ABJECT	FACETIOUS	ORBS
AGUE	HEEDLESS	PERFUNCTORY
ALTERCATION	IMPENDING	PLACIDLY
AUDACIOUS	IMPETUS	PONDEROUS
BLITHE	IMPRECATIONS	PRODIGIOUS
CHAOS	INDIGNANTLY	RELIANCE
CONDESCENSION	INTERMINABLE	REPOSE
DAUNTLESS	LUDICROUS	REPROOF
DELIRIUM	MOROSE	SINUOUS
DENOTED	OBDURATE	SMITTEN
DENUNCIATION	OBLIGED	SPECTER
DISCERNED	OBSCURITY	SULLEN
ELATION	OMINOUS	

Red Badge of Courage Vocabulary Word Search 4

Words are placed backwards, forward, diagonally, up and down. Words listed below are included in the maze. Circle the hidden vocabulary words in the maze.

```
V A N Q U I S H E D D N P L D D F D D
H H O R S P U S L Y E P E U E O I E
V C I X E V O X A T G R R D N N R S S
R R T W K L N X T W I O F I U O M C P
B F C J L J I I P L D U C N T I E O
R E I C L S M A O S B I N R C D R N
X N D Z O S O N N J O G C O I D A N D
F N E R R N D Z X C B I T U A D B E E
A T L S A E D F N P E O O S T E L D N
C W A Q R G F E K L W U R R I L E K T
E C M O T M G F S A B S Y N O I H L S
T X U T S O X L Z C G K J S N R F U D
I S A H F R X M E I E J F E H I O M I
O V C S S O Q T Q D S N S H W U S I S
U B C P P S C F B L V H S T N M B M C
S D I M P E T U S Y T I M I X O R P O
H K C M J W R F B G S F S L O E O E N
G W H B Q B H A T G T U S B T N R N C
E T A R U D B O T S K Q L C Q G E D E
A F O O B S C U R I T Y E L D T P I R
V G S S E L D E E H O P H F E K O N T
D A U D A C I O U S S N W B P N S G E
A L T E R C A T I O N F O O R P E R D
```

ABJECT	ELATION	ORBS
AGUE	EXASPERATION	PERFUNCTORY
ALTERCATION	FACETIOUS	PLACIDLY
AUDACIOUS	FORMIDABLE	PONDEROUS
BEDRAGGLED	HEEDLESS	PRODIGIOUS
BLITHE	IMPENDING	PROXIMITY
CHAOS	IMPETUS	RELIANCE
CONDESCENSION	LUDICROUS	REPOSE
DELIRIUM	MALEDICTION	REPROOF
DENOTED	MOROSE	SINUOUS
DENUNCIATION	OBDURATE	SMITTEN
DESPONDENT	OBLIGED	SPECTER
DISCERNED	OBSCURITY	SULLEN
DISCONCERTED	OMINOUS	VANQUISHED

92
Copyrighted

Red Badge of Courage Vocabulary Word Search 4 Answer Key

Words are placed backwards, forward, diagonally, up and down. Words listed below are included in the maze. Circle the hidden vocabulary words in the maze.

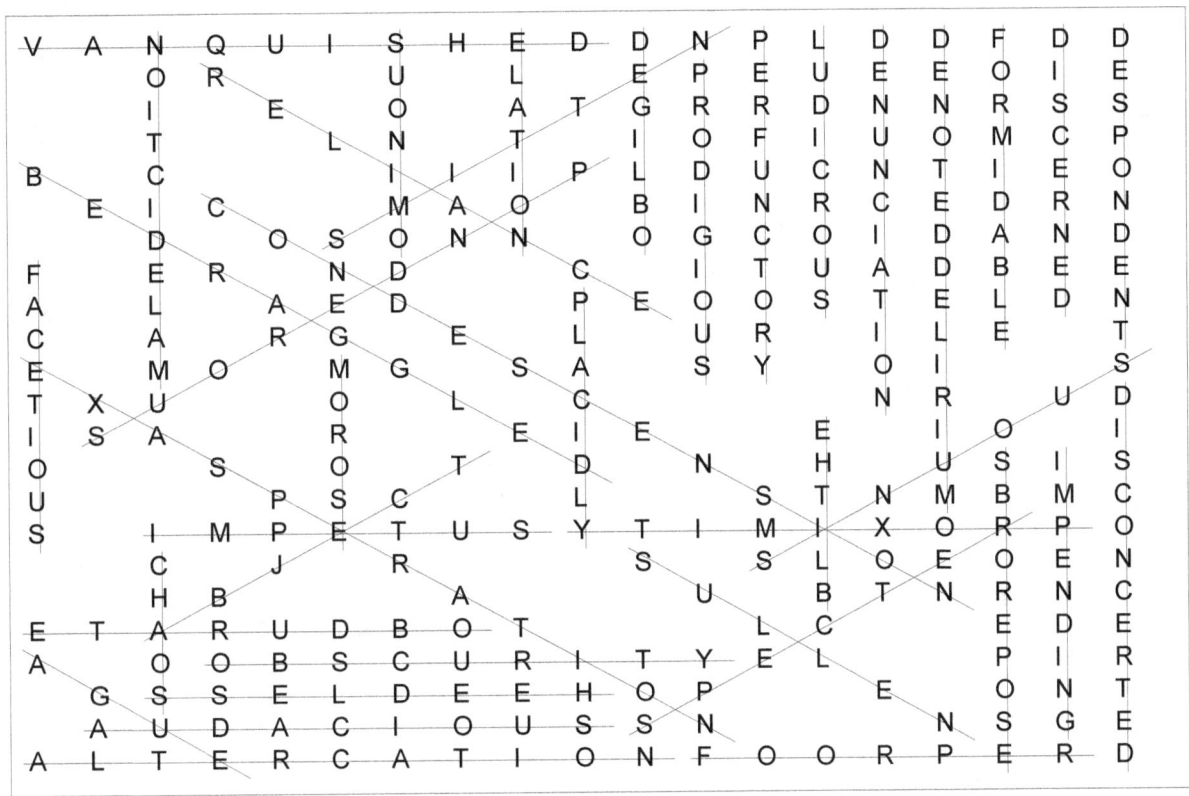

ABJECT	ELATION	ORBS
AGUE	EXASPERATION	PERFUNCTORY
ALTERCATION	FACETIOUS	PLACIDLY
AUDACIOUS	FORMIDABLE	PONDEROUS
BEDRAGGLED	HEEDLESS	PRODIGIOUS
BLITHE	IMPENDING	PROXIMITY
CHAOS	IMPETUS	RELIANCE
CONDESCENSION	LUDICROUS	REPOSE
DELIRIUM	MALEDICTION	REPROOF
DENOTED	MOROSE	SINUOUS
DENUNCIATION	OBDURATE	SMITTEN
DESPONDENT	OBLIGED	SPECTER
DISCERNED	OBSCURITY	SULLEN
DISCONCERTED	OMINOUS	VANQUISHED

Red Badge of Courage Vocabulary Crossword 1

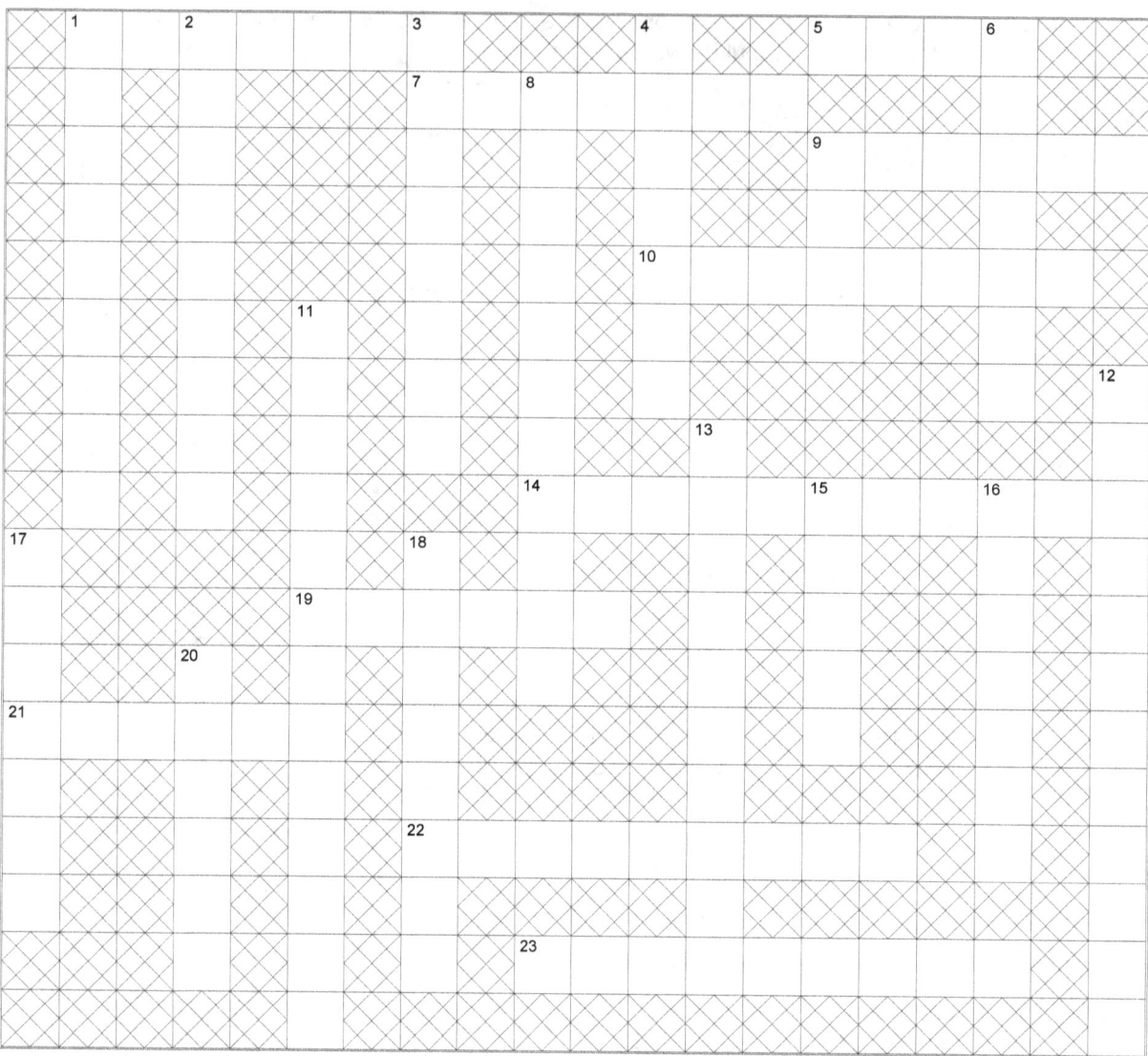

Across
1. Caused to do something
5. Eyes
7. Exalted feeling arising from a sense of triumph, power or relief
9. Wretched; of the most contemptible kind
10. Intractable; not giving in
14. Heating or noisy quarrel
19. Morose, sulky
21. Rest
22. Fearless; bold
23. Massive

Down
1. The condition of being unknown
2. Laughable because of obvious absurdity or incongruity
3. Temporary mental confusion
4. Winding
6. Ghost; phantasm
8. Wiped out; destroyed completely
9. A recurrent chill or fit of shivering
11. The act of coming down voluntarily to the level of inferiors
12. An open condemnation or censure
13. Made wet and limp
15. Total disorder or confusion
16. Impelling force; impulse; stimulus
17. Reprimand
18. Outwardly calm or composed; complacent
20. Melancholy; gloomy; ill-humored

Red Badge of Courage Vocabulary Crossword 1 Answer Key

	1 O	2 B	L	I	G	E	3 D			4 S		5 O	R	B	6 S	
	B	U					7 E	8 L	A	T	I	O	N		P	
	S	D					L	N		N		9 A	B	J	E	C	T
	C	I					I	N		U		G			C	
	U	C					R	I		10 O	B	D	U	R	A	T	E
	R	R		11 C		I		H		U		E			E	
	I	O		O		U		I		S					R	12 D
	T	U		N		M		L			13 B					E
	Y	S		D				14 A	L	T	E	R	15 C	A	16 T	I	O	N
17 R				E		18 P		T			D		H		M		U
E				19 S	U	L	L	E	N		R		A		P		N
P		20 M		C		A		D			A		O		E		C
21 R	E	P	O	S	E		C				G		S		T		I
O		R		N			I				G				U		A
O		O		S			22 D	A	U	N	T	L	E	S	S		T
F		S		I			L				E						I
		E		O			Y		23 P	O	N	D	E	R	O	U	S	O
				N													N

Across
1. Caused to do something
5. Eyes
7. Exalted feeling arising from a sense of triumph, power or relief
9. Wretched; of the most contemptible kind
10. Intractable; not giving in
14. Heating or noisy quarrel
19. Morose, sulky
21. Rest
22. Fearless; bold
23. Massive

Down
1. The condition of being unknown
2. Laughable because of obvious absurdity or incongruity
3. Temporary mental confusion
4. Winding
6. Ghost; phantasm
8. Wiped out; destroyed completely
9. A recurrent chill or fit of shivering
11. The act of coming down voluntarily to the level of inferiors
12. An open condemnation or censure
13. Made wet and limp
15. Total disorder or confusion
16. Impelling force; impulse; stimulus
17. Reprimand
18. Outwardly calm or composed; complacent
20. Melancholy; gloomy; ill-humored

Red Badge of Courage Vocabulary Crossword 2

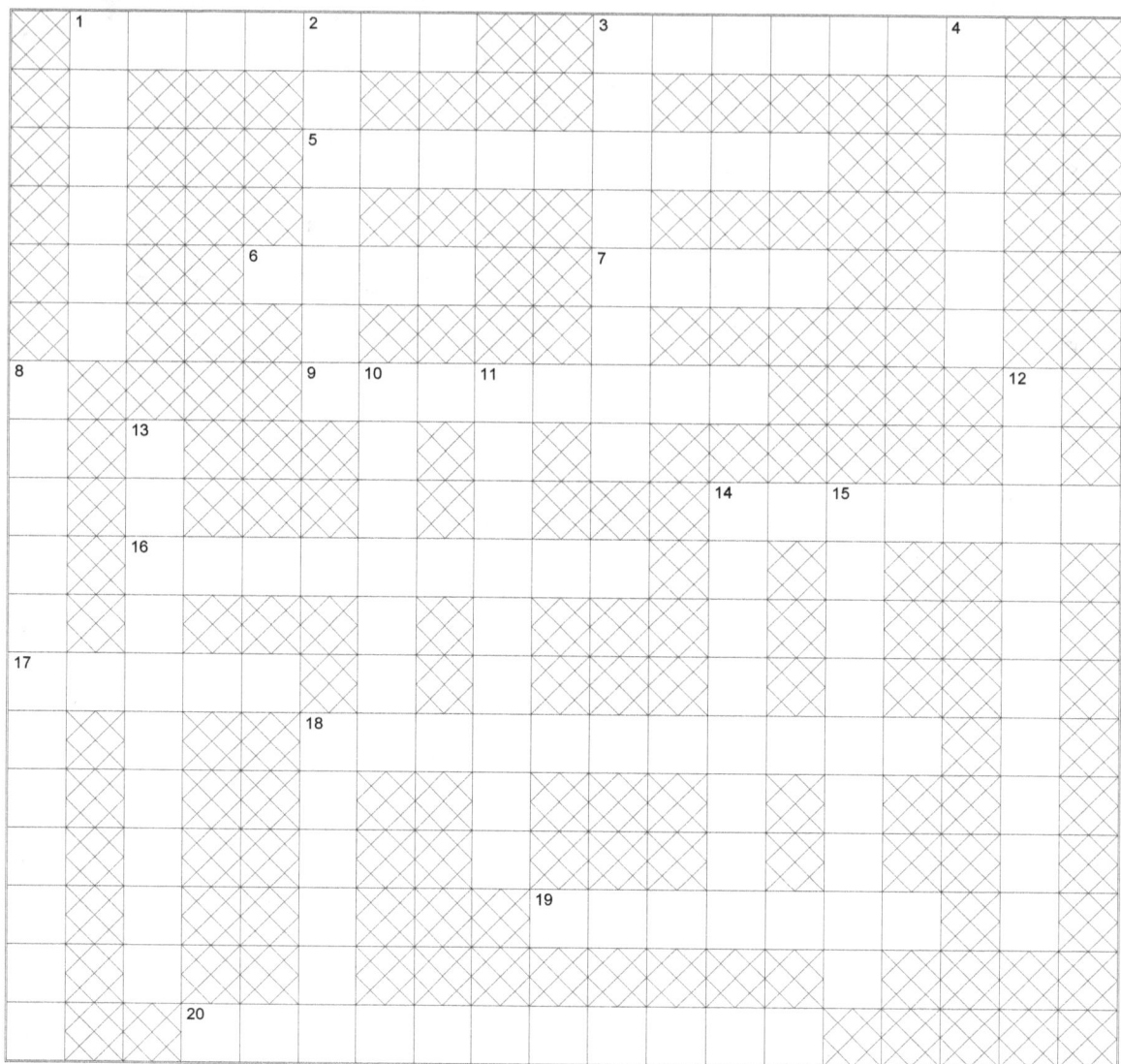

Across
1. Winding
3. Ghost; phantasm
5. Laughable because of obvious absurdity or incongruity
6. A recurrent chill or fit of shivering
7. Eyes
9. Temporary mental confusion
14. Reprimand
16. Fearless; bold
17. Total disorder or confusion
18. Wiped out; destroyed completely
19. Impelling force; impulse; stimulus
20. Heating or noisy quarrel

Down
1. Morose, sulky
2. Caused to do something
3. Mocking; cynical
4. Rest
8. An open condemnation or censure
10. Exalted feeling arising from a sense of triumph, power or relief
11. Likely to happen soon
12. Enormous, extraordinary; marvelous
13. Made wet and limp
14. Confidence; dependence; trust
15. Massive
18. Wretched; of the most contemptible kind

Red Badge of Courage Vocabulary Crossword 2 Answer Key

Across
1. Winding
3. Ghost; phantasm
5. Laughable because of obvious absurdity or incongruity
6. A recurrent chill or fit of shivering
7. Eyes
9. Temporary mental confusion
14. Reprimand
16. Fearless; bold
17. Total disorder or confusion
18. Wiped out; destroyed completely
19. Impelling force; impulse; stimulus
20. Heating or noisy quarrel

Down
1. Morose, sulky
2. Caused to do something
3. Mocking; cynical
4. Rest
8. An open condemnation or censure
10. Exalted feeling arising from a sense of triumph, power or relief
11. Likely to happen soon
12. Enormous, extraordinary; marvelous
13. Made wet and limp
14. Confidence; dependence; trust
15. Massive
18. Wretched; of the most contemptible kind

Red Badge of Courage Vocabulary Crossword 3

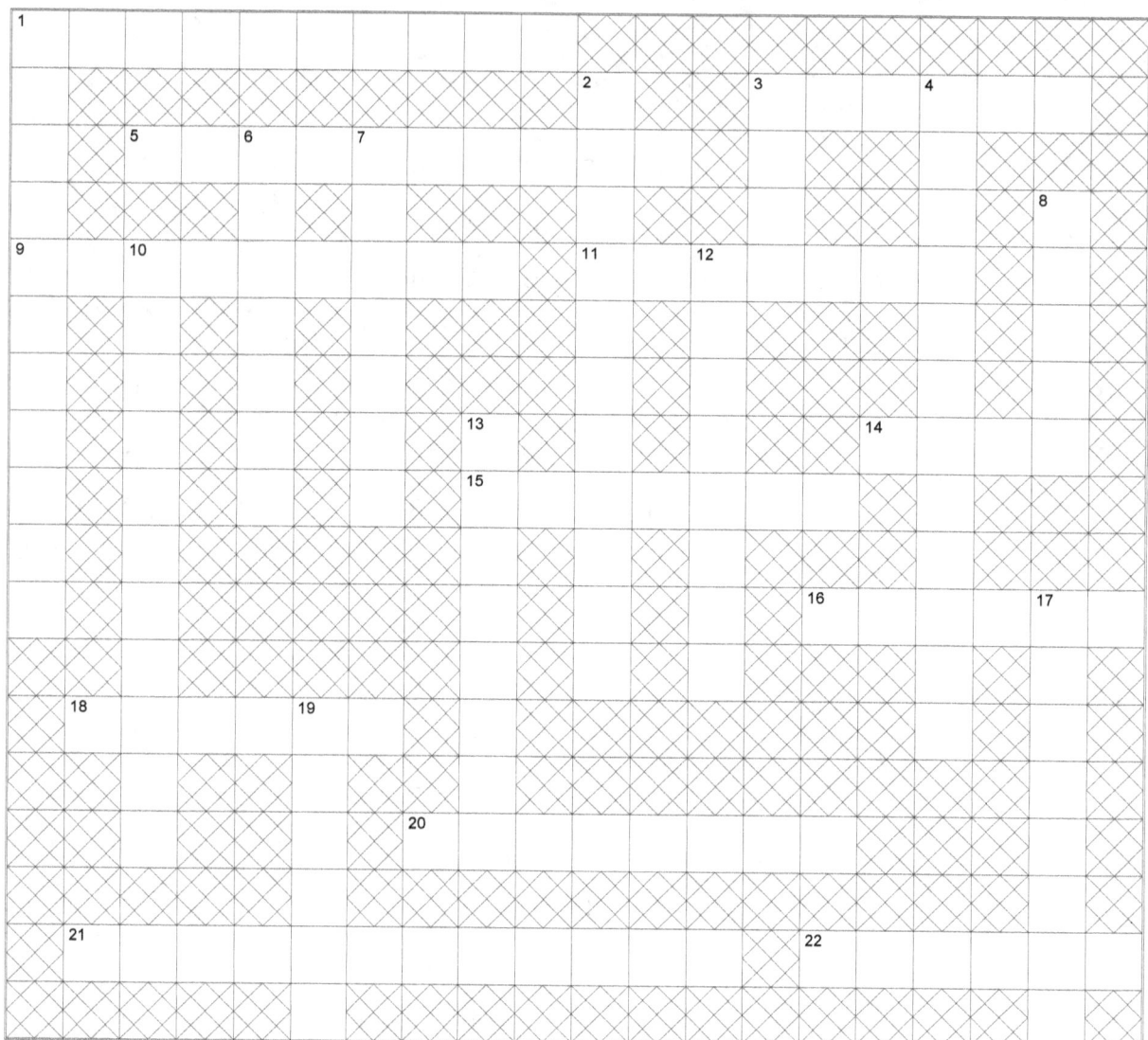

Across
1. Defeated; overcome
3. Wretched; of the most contemptible kind
5. Feeling disheartened or dejected
9. Likely to happen soon
11. Impelling force; impulse; stimulus
14. Eyes
15. Exalted feeling arising from a sense of triumph, power or relief
16. Cheerful; casual; carefree
18. Melancholy; gloomy; ill-humored
20. Temporary mental confusion
21. Curses
22. Rest

Down
1. The evidence or argument that justifies an act
2. Wiped out; destroyed completely
3. A recurrent chill or fit of shivering
4. The state of extremely annoyed or irritated
6. Winding
7. Portentous; foreboding
8. Total disorder or confusion
10. Acting with little interest or care
12. Outwardly calm or composed; complacent
13. Confidence; dependence; trust
17. Paying little or no attention; unmindful
19. Morose, sulky

Red Badge of Courage Vocabulary Crossword 3 Answer Key

Across
1. Defeated; overcome
3. Wretched; of the most contemptible kind
5. Feeling disheartened or dejected
9. Likely to happen soon
11. Impelling force; impulse; stimulus
14. Eyes
15. Exalted feeling arising from a sense of triumph, power or relief
16. Cheerful; casual; carefree
18. Melancholy; gloomy; ill-humored
20. Temporary mental confusion
21. Curses
22. Rest

Down
1. The evidence or argument that justifies an act
2. Wiped out; destroyed completely
3. A recurrent chill or fit of shivering
4. The state of extremely annoyed or irritated
6. Winding
7. Portentous; foreboding
8. Total disorder or confusion
10. Acting with little interest or care
12. Outwardly calm or composed; complacent
13. Confidence; dependence; trust
17. Paying little or no attention; unmindful
19. Morose, sulky

Red Badge of Courage Vocabulary Crossword 4

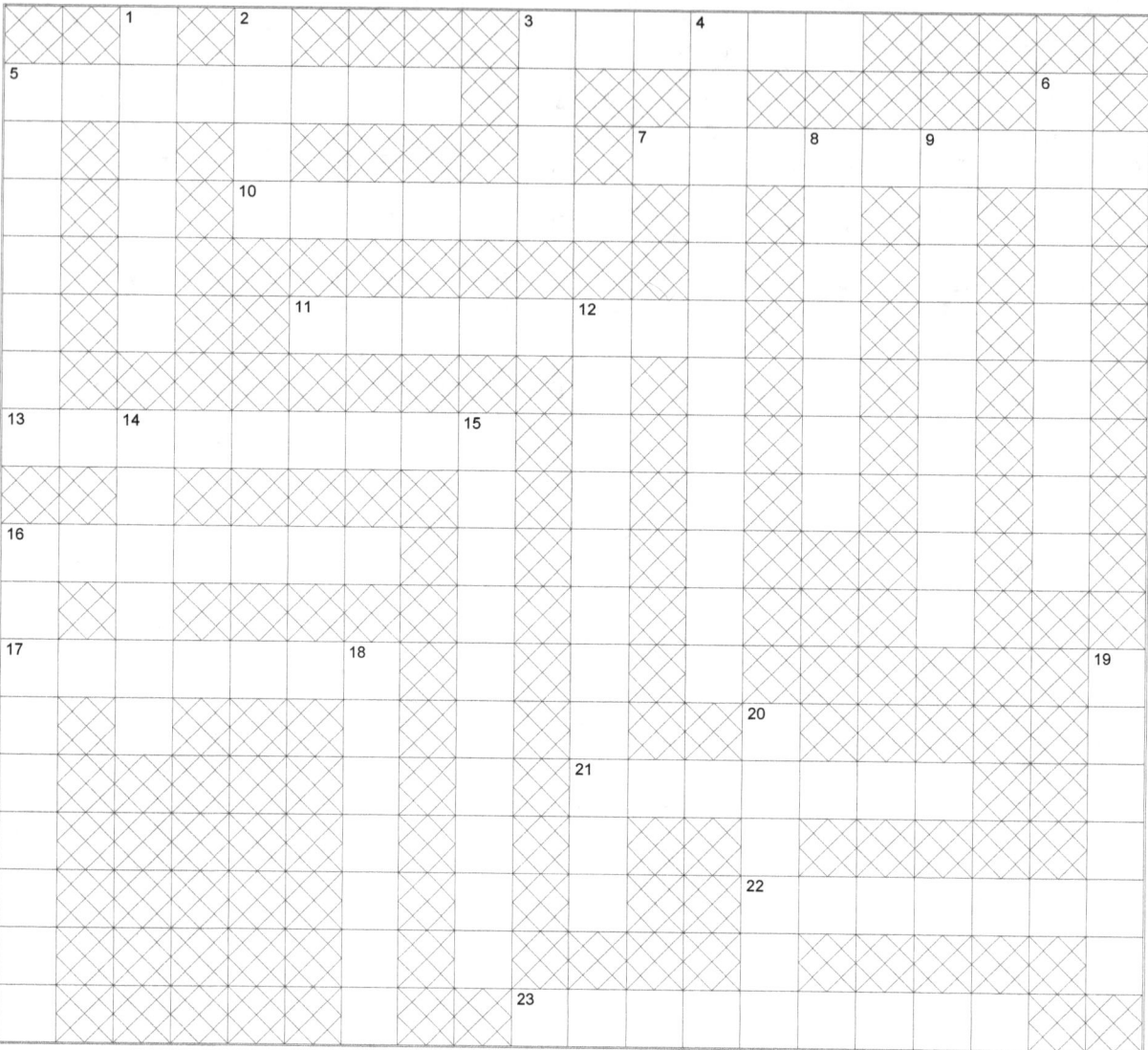

Across
3. Wretched; of the most contemptible kind
5. Temporary mental confusion
7. Humorous and flippant; playfully jocular
10. Afflicted
11. Intractable; not giving in
13. Detected; perceived
16. Caused to do something
17. Ghost; phantasm
21. Impelling force; impulse; stimulus
22. Portentous; foreboding
23. Massive

Down
1. Cheerful; casual; carefree
2. Eyes
3. A recurrent chill or fit of shivering
4. The state of extremely annoyed or irritated
5. Marked; indicated; signified
6. Laughable because of obvious absurdity or incongruity
8. Exalted feeling arising from a sense of triumph, power or relief
9. Likely to happen soon
12. Heating or noisy quarrel
14. Morose, sulky
15. Feeling disheartened or dejected
16. The condition of being unknown
18. Reprimand
19. Melancholy; gloomy; ill-humored
20. Rest

Red Badge of Courage Vocabulary Crossword 4 Answer Key

		1 B		2 O			3 A	B	J	4 E	C	T			
5 D	E	L	I	R	I	U	M			X				6 L	
E		I		B			U		7 F	A	8 C	E	9 T	I	O	U	S
N		T		10 S	M	I	T	T	E	N	S		L		M		D	
O		H							P		A		P		I	
T		E		11 O	B	D	U	R	12 A	T	E		T		E		C	
E									L		R		I		N		R	
13 D	14 I	S	C	E	R	N	15 E	D		T		A		O		D		O	
	S					U		E			E		T		N		I		U	
16 O	B	L	I	G	E	D		S		R		I			N		S	
B		L						P		C		O			G			
17 S	P	E	C	T	E	R		18 R		O		A		N				19 M
C		N						E		T				20 R				O
U								P				21 I	M	P	E	T	U	S	R
R								R		E				P				O
I								O		N				22 O	M	I	N	O	U	S
T								O		T				S				E
Y								F		23 P	O	N	D	E	R	O	U	S

Across
3. Wretched; of the most contemptible kind
5. Temporary mental confusion
7. Humorous and flippant; playfully jocular
10. Afflicted
11. Intractable; not giving in
13. Detected; perceived
16. Caused to do something
17. Ghost; phantasm
21. Impelling force; impulse; stimulus
22. Portentous; foreboding
23. Massive

Down
1. Cheerful; casual; carefree
2. Eyes
3. A recurrent chill or fit of shivering
4. The state of extremely annoyed or irritated
5. Marked; indicated; signified
6. Laughable because of obvious absurdity or incongruity
8. Exalted feeling arising from a sense of triumph, power or relief
9. Likely to happen soon
12. Heating or noisy quarrel
14. Morose, sulky
15. Feeling disheartened or dejected
16. The condition of being unknown
18. Reprimand
19. Melancholy; gloomy; ill-humored
20. Rest

Red Badge of Courage Vocabulary Juggle Letters 1

1. ENMTTIS = 1. _____
   Afflicted

2. ETCOUASFI = 2. _____
   Humorous and flippant; playfully jocular

3. ETSCPRE = 3. _____
   Ghost; phantasm

4. OSNIOMU = 4. _____
   Portentous; foreboding

5. OSCHA = 5. _____
   Total disorder or confusion

6. ETLUSANSD = 6. _____
   Fearless; bold

7. CICRTNDEEDOS = 7. _____
   Lacking self-composure

8. HESSEDLE = 8. _____
   Paying little or no attention; unmindful

9. ERANECIL = 9. _____
   Confidence; dependence; trust

10. ORTCYFPRUNE =10. _____
    Acting with little interest or care

11. TCEMLIDNIAO =11. _____
    A curse or slander

12. NEALTTACOIR =12. _____
    Heating or noisy quarrel

13. IINNDTACVIO =13. _____
    The evidence or argument that justifies an act

14. ENTDODE =14. _____
    Marked; indicated; signified

15. OGIOSIURDP =15. _____
    Enormous, extraordinary; marvelous

Red Badge of Courage Vocabulary Juggle Letters 1 Answer Key

1. ENMTTIS = 1. SMITTEN
Afflicted

2. ETCOUASFI = 2. FACETIOUS
Humorous and flippant; playfully jocular

3. ETSCPRE = 3. SPECTER
Ghost; phantasm

4. OSNIOMU = 4. OMINOUS
Portentous; foreboding

5. OSCHA = 5. CHAOS
Total disorder or confusion

6. ETLUSANSD = 6. DAUNTLESS
Fearless; bold

7. CICRTNDEEDOS = 7. DISCONCERTED
Lacking self-composure

8. HESSEDLE = 8. HEEDLESS
Paying little or no attention; unmindful

9. ERANECIL = 9. RELIANCE
Confidence; dependence; trust

10. ORTCYFPRUNE = 10. PERFUNCTORY
Acting with little interest or care

11. TCEMLIDNIAO = 11. MALEDICTION
A curse or slander

12. NEALTTACOIR = 12. ALTERCATION
Heating or noisy quarrel

13. IINNDTACVIO = 13. VINDICATION
The evidence or argument that justifies an act

14. ENTDODE = 14. DENOTED
Marked; indicated; signified

15. OGIOSIURDP = 15. PRODIGIOUS
Enormous, extraordinary; marvelous

Red Badge of Courage Vocabulary Juggle Letters 2

1. LAMDBRIFOE = 1. _____
   Arousing fear or dread; awesome; difficult to overtake

2. OSNEEDNTDP = 2. _____
   Feeling disheartened or dejected

3. DDAEGGRBEL = 3. _____
   Made wet and limp

4. UHVNIDEQSA = 4. _____
   Defeated; overcome

5. ROCTISYUB = 5. _____
   The condition of being unknown

6. METNERIIBLAN = 6. _____
   Endless

7. ILYCLDPA = 7. _____
   Outwardly calm or composed; complacent

8. UIRIELDM = 8. _____
   Temporary mental confusion

9. SRBO = 9. _____
   Eyes

10. EUDNITNACNOI =10. _____
    An open condemnation or censure

11. CLDRSIOUU =11. _____
    Laughable because of obvious absurdity or incongruity

12. ROEORFP =12. _____
    Reprimand

13. IDCUASAUO =13. _____
    Arrogantly insolent

14. NATDLEOCIIM =14. _____
    A curse or slander

15. TENEDDO =15. _____
    Marked; indicated; signified

Red Badge of Courage Vocabulary Juggle Letters 2 Answer Key

1. LAMDBRIFOE = 1. FORMIDABLE
   Arousing fear or dread; awesome; difficult to overtake

2. OSNEEDNTDP = 2. DESPONDENT
   Feeling disheartened or dejected

3. DDAEGGRBEL = 3. BEDRAGGLED
   Made wet and limp

4. UHVNIDEQSA = 4. VANQUISHED
   Defeated; overcome

5. ROCTISYUB = 5. OBSCURITY
   The condition of being unknown

6. METNERIIBLAN = 6. INTERMINABLE
   Endless

7. ILYCLDPA = 7. PLACIDLY
   Outwardly calm or composed; complacent

8. UIRIELDM = 8. DELIRIUM
   Temporary mental confusion

9. SRBO = 9. ORBS
   Eyes

10. EUDNITNACNOI = 10. DENUNCIATION
    An open condemnation or censure

11. CLDRSIOUU = 11. LUDICROUS
    Laughable because of obvious absurdity or incongruity

12. ROEORFP = 12. REPROOF
    Reprimand

13. IDCUASAUO = 13. AUDACIOUS
    Arrogantly insolent

14. NATDLEOCIIM = 14. MALEDICTION
    A curse or slander

15. TENEDDO = 15. DENOTED
    Marked; indicated; signified

Red Badge of Courage Vocabulary Juggle Letters 3

1. MLTAERBIENNI = 1. _____
   Endless

2. DANIANLEITH = 2. _____
   Wiped out; destroyed completely

3. EOPRFOR = 3. _____
   Reprimand

4. SREOEP = 4. _____
   Rest

5. PIINDNEMG = 5. _____
   Likely to happen soon

6. AUDAIOUCS = 6. _____
   Arrogantly insolent

7. SERCCEOTNDDI = 7. _____
   Lacking self-composure

8. EUAFCSITO = 8. _____
   Humorous and flippant; playfully jocular

9. TNSTEMI = 9. _____
   Afflicted

10. SUDOOEPNR =10. _____
    Massive

11. HASUVDENIQ =11. _____
    Defeated; overcome

12. ALEECINR =12. _____
    Confidence; dependence; trust

13. CUIYRBSTO =13. _____
    The condition of being unknown

14. MNOUOIS =14. _____
    Portentous; foreboding

15. RPMOTIYIX =15. _____
    Closeness

Red Badge of Courage Vocabulary Juggle Letters 3 Answer Key

1. MLTAERBIENNI = 1. INTERMINABLE
   Endless

2. DANIANLEITH = 2. ANNIHILATED
   Wiped out; destroyed completely

3. EOPRFOR = 3. REPROOF
   Reprimand

4. SREOEP = 4. REPOSE
   Rest

5. PIINDNEMG = 5. IMPENDING
   Likely to happen soon

6. AUDAIOUCS = 6. AUDACIOUS
   Arrogantly insolent

7. SERCCEOTNDDI = 7. DISCONCERTED
   Lacking self-composure

8. EUAFCSITO = 8. FACETIOUS
   Humorous and flippant; playfully jocular

9. TNSTEMI = 9. SMITTEN
   Afflicted

10. SUDOOEPNR =10. PONDEROUS
    Massive

11. HASUVDENIQ =11. VANQUISHED
    Defeated; overcome

12. ALEECINR =12. RELIANCE
    Confidence; dependence; trust

13. CUIYRBSTO =13. OBSCURITY
    The condition of being unknown

14. MNOUOIS =14. OMINOUS
    Portentous; foreboding

15. RPMOTIYIX =15. PROXIMITY
    Closeness

Red Badge of Courage Vocabulary Juggle Letters 4

1. IOGUIPRSDO = 1. _____
   Enormous, extraordinary; marvelous

2. OROSEM = 2. _____
   Melancholy; gloomy; ill-humored

3. DNRICOAS = 3. _____
   Mocking; cynical

4. GUAE = 4. _____
   A recurrent chill or fit of shivering

5. CADNNOIIVTI = 5. _____
   The evidence or argument that justifies an act

6. NVAQDEHISU = 6. _____
   Defeated; overcome

7. USOUISN = 7. _____
   Winding

8. ROERPOF = 8. _____
   Reprimand

9. DRCSNIEDE = 9. _____
   Detected; perceived

10. EDTSUSLNA = 10. _____
    Fearless; bold

11. GPIIMENND = 11. _____
    Likely to happen soon

12. RLIMEIUD = 12. _____
    Temporary mental confusion

13. BRUAODET = 13. _____
    Intractable; not giving in

14. OSENDETPND = 14. _____
    Feeling disheartened or dejected

15. DEOGLBI = 15. _____
    Caused to do something

Red Badge of Courage Vocabulary Juggle Letters 4 Answer Key

1. IOGUIPRSDO = 1. PRODIGIOUS
Enormous, extraordinary; marvelous

2. OROSEM = 2. MOROSE
Melancholy; gloomy; ill-humored

3. DNRICOAS = 3. SARDONIC
Mocking; cynical

4. GUAE = 4. AGUE
A recurrent chill or fit of shivering

5. CADNNOIIVTI = 5. VINDICATION
The evidence or argument that justifies an act

6. NVAQDEHISU = 6. VANQUISHED
Defeated; overcome

7. USOUISN = 7. SINUOUS
Winding

8. ROERPOF = 8. REPROOF
Reprimand

9. DRCSNIEDE = 9. DISCERNED
Detected; perceived

10. EDTSUSLNA =10. DAUNTLESS
Fearless; bold

11. GPIIMENND =11. IMPENDING
Likely to happen soon

12. RLIMEIUD =12. DELIRIUM
Temporary mental confusion

13. BRUAODET =13. OBDURATE
Intractable; not giving in

14. OSENDETPND =14. DESPONDENT
Feeling disheartened or dejected

15. DEOGLBI =15. OBLIGED
Caused to do something

ABJECT	Wretched; of the most contemptible kind
AGUE	A recurrent chill or fit of shivering
ALTERCATION	Heating or noisy quarrel
ANNIHILATED	Wiped out; destroyed completely
AUDACIOUS	Arrogantly insolent

BEDRAGGLED	Made wet and limp
BLITHE	Cheerful; casual; carefree
CHAOS	Total disorder or confusion
CONDESCENSION	The act of coming down voluntarily to the level of inferiors
DAUNTLESS	Fearless; bold

DELIRIUM	Temporary mental confusion
DENOTED	Marked; indicated; signified
DENUNCIATION	An open condemnation or censure
DESPONDENT	Feeling disheartened or dejected
DISCERNED	Detected; perceived

DISCONCERTED	Lacking self-composure
ELATION	Exalted feeling arising from a sense of triumph, power or relief
EXASPERATION	The state of extremely annoyed or irritated
FACETIOUS	Humorous and flippant; playfully jocular
FORMIDABLE	Arousing fear or dread; awesome; difficult to overtake

HEEDLESS	Paying little or no attention; unmindful
IMPENDING	Likely to happen soon
IMPETUS	Impelling force; impulse; stimulus
IMPRECATIONS	Curses
INDIGNANTLY	With an anger aroused by something unjust

INTERMINABLE	Endless
LUDICROUS	Laughable because of obvious absurdity or incongruity
MALEDICTION	A curse or slander
MOROSE	Melancholy; gloomy; ill-humored
OBDURATE	Intractable; not giving in

OBLIGED	Caused to do something
OBSCURITY	The condition of being unknown
OMINOUS	Portentous; foreboding
ORBS	Eyes
PERFUNCTORY	Acting with little interest or care

PLACIDLY	Outwardly calm or composed; complacent
PONDEROUS	Massive
PRODIGIOUS	Enormous, extraordinary; marvelous
PROXIMITY	Closeness
RELIANCE	Confidence; dependence; trust

REPOSE	Rest
REPROOF	Reprimand
SARDONIC	Mocking; cynical
SINUOUS	Winding
SMITTEN	Afflicted

SPECTER	Ghost; phantasm
SULLEN	Morose, sulky
VANQUISHED	Defeated; overcome
VINDICATION	The evidence or argument that justifies an act

Red Badge of Courage Vocab

OBDURATE	OBLIGED	PROXIMITY	AUDACIOUS	REPROOF
MALEDICTION	VINDICATION	REPOSE	OBSCURITY	ORBS
IMPRECATIONS	PERFUNCTORY	FREE SPACE	PLACIDLY	IMPETUS
CHAOS	SMITTEN	PRODIGIOUS	BEDRAGGLED	DAUNTLESS
FORMIDABLE	INDIGNANTLY	BLITHE	SINUOUS	OMINOUS

Red Badge of Courage Vocab

CONDESCENSION	LUDICROUS	VANQUISHED	HEEDLESS	PONDEROUS
ABJECT	IMPENDING	MOROSE	EXASPERATION	SULLEN
DELIRIUM	INTERMINABLE	FREE SPACE	DENUNCIATION	ALTERCATION
ANNIHILATED	DISCONCERTED	AGUE	DENOTED	SARDONIC
RELIANCE	DESPONDENT	SPECTER	ELATION	OMINOUS

Red Badge of Courage Vocab

IMPENDING	AGUE	HEEDLESS	FORMIDABLE	ANNIHILATED
OMINOUS	RELIANCE	ALTERCATION	IMPETUS	VINDICATION
ABJECT	VANQUISHED	FREE SPACE	REPOSE	DISCERNED
OBLIGED	CHAOS	DELIRIUM	SMITTEN	PROXIMITY
CONDESCENSION	DENOTED	INTERMINABLE	BEDRAGGLED	MOROSE

Red Badge of Courage Vocab

PERFUNCTORY	DESPONDENT	MALEDICTION	EXASPERATION	ELATION
DISCONCERTED	DENUNCIATION	SPECTER	BLITHE	INDIGNANTLY
LUDICROUS	SINUOUS	FREE SPACE	AUDACIOUS	OBDURATE
SULLEN	ORBS	PLACIDLY	SARDONIC	REPROOF
PRODIGIOUS	OBSCURITY	DAUNTLESS	PONDEROUS	MOROSE

Red Badge of Courage Vocab

DENUNCIATION	RELIANCE	FACETIOUS	PRODIGIOUS	IMPRECATIONS
ALTERCATION	OBSCURITY	ABJECT	LUDICROUS	DELIRIUM
AGUE	ELATION	FREE SPACE	VANQUISHED	SMITTEN
OMINOUS	OBLIGED	ORBS	EXASPERATION	MALEDICTION
SINUOUS	SULLEN	FORMIDABLE	CHAOS	PLACIDLY

Red Badge of Courage Vocab

INDIGNANTLY	REPROOF	PROXIMITY	PERFUNCTORY	INTERMINABLE
VINDICATION	DENOTED	HEEDLESS	AUDACIOUS	SARDONIC
DESPONDENT	BEDRAGGLED	FREE SPACE	PONDEROUS	DISCERNED
CONDESCENSION	DISCONCERTED	IMPETUS	ANNIHILATED	REPOSE
MOROSE	OBDURATE	SPECTER	IMPENDING	PLACIDLY

Red Badge of Courage Vocab

ALTERCATION	PONDEROUS	PLACIDLY	DISCONCERTED	DENOTED
IMPENDING	EXASPERATION	SINUOUS	SULLEN	MALEDICTION
SMITTEN	OBSCURITY	FREE SPACE	VANQUISHED	OBLIGED
SARDONIC	IMPRECATIONS	INTERMINABLE	MOROSE	DISCERNED
IMPETUS	PERFUNCTORY	HEEDLESS	BEDRAGGLED	RELIANCE

Red Badge of Courage Vocab

SPECTER	ELATION	OBDURATE	PRODIGIOUS	DESPONDENT
AGUE	OMINOUS	BLITHE	FACETIOUS	ANNIHILATED
INDIGNANTLY	ORBS	FREE SPACE	PROXIMITY	REPROOF
DENUNCIATION	VINDICATION	CHAOS	REPOSE	FORMIDABLE
DELIRIUM	DAUNTLESS	LUDICROUS	ABJECT	RELIANCE

Red Badge of Courage Vocab

IMPENDING	MOROSE	FORMIDABLE	HEEDLESS	DESPONDENT
VINDICATION	SPECTER	REPOSE	LUDICROUS	PONDEROUS
IMPRECATIONS	EXASPERATION	FREE SPACE	CHAOS	FACETIOUS
ABJECT	SULLEN	AUDACIOUS	ORBS	DISCERNED
DAUNTLESS	OBSCURITY	SMITTEN	OBDURATE	ALTERCATION

Red Badge of Courage Vocab

PERFUNCTORY	MALEDICTION	PROXIMITY	REPROOF	DISCONCERTED
OBLIGED	DELIRIUM	INDIGNANTLY	VANQUISHED	ELATION
INTERMINABLE	DENOTED	FREE SPACE	SARDONIC	PLACIDLY
RELIANCE	BLITHE	AGUE	IMPETUS	DENUNCIATION
SINUOUS	OMINOUS	ANNIHILATED	BEDRAGGLED	ALTERCATION

Red Badge of Courage Vocab

AUDACIOUS	ORBS	DISCONCERTED	CHAOS	FACETIOUS
CONDESCENSION	DENUNCIATION	MALEDICTION	BLITHE	REPOSE
SULLEN	SPECTER	FREE SPACE	IMPENDING	DELIRIUM
DAUNTLESS	RELIANCE	FORMIDABLE	ABJECT	BEDRAGGLED
PLACIDLY	DESPONDENT	SARDONIC	ELATION	ANNIHILATED

Red Badge of Courage Vocab

PONDEROUS	EXASPERATION	ALTERCATION	OBLIGED	HEEDLESS
DISCERNED	VANQUISHED	OMINOUS	SINUOUS	AGUE
LUDICROUS	OBDURATE	FREE SPACE	MOROSE	IMPRECATIONS
PERFUNCTORY	SMITTEN	INDIGNANTLY	DENOTED	PROXIMITY
VINDICATION	PRODIGIOUS	IMPETUS	REPROOF	ANNIHILATED

Red Badge of Courage Vocab

ALTERCATION	CONDESCENSION	BEDRAGGLED	INTERMINABLE	AGUE
OBDURATE	PROXIMITY	ELATION	SMITTEN	LUDICROUS
ORBS	MALEDICTION	FREE SPACE	IMPENDING	BLITHE
RELIANCE	DISCERNED	OBLIGED	HEEDLESS	REPOSE
INDIGNANTLY	IMPRECATIONS	CHAOS	ABJECT	DISCONCERTED

Red Badge of Courage Vocab

FORMIDABLE	REPROOF	DENUNCIATION	PLACIDLY	DELIRIUM
DENOTED	PERFUNCTORY	OBSCURITY	SARDONIC	DESPONDENT
ANNIHILATED	MOROSE	FREE SPACE	OMINOUS	AUDACIOUS
DAUNTLESS	VANQUISHED	PRODIGIOUS	SINUOUS	SULLEN
PONDEROUS	SPECTER	EXASPERATION	FACETIOUS	DISCONCERTED

Red Badge of Courage Vocab

BLITHE	IMPETUS	CONDESCENSION	ABJECT	DELIRIUM
ORBS	DISCERNED	BEDRAGGLED	FORMIDABLE	DENOTED
IMPENDING	REPROOF	FREE SPACE	OBSCURITY	OBDURATE
EXASPERATION	AGUE	SULLEN	OMINOUS	SINUOUS
SMITTEN	ELATION	IMPRECATIONS	SPECTER	PROXIMITY

Red Badge of Courage Vocab

DAUNTLESS	INTERMINABLE	FACETIOUS	MALEDICTION	SARDONIC
PERFUNCTORY	ANNIHILATED	INDIGNANTLY	DENUNCIATION	PRODIGIOUS
VINDICATION	PONDEROUS	FREE SPACE	VANQUISHED	HEEDLESS
REPOSE	CHAOS	LUDICROUS	PLACIDLY	DISCONCERTED
DESPONDENT	RELIANCE	MOROSE	ALTERCATION	PROXIMITY

Red Badge of Courage Vocab

DELIRIUM	REPOSE	SMITTEN	BLITHE	ORBS
OBSCURITY	SARDONIC	FORMIDABLE	ABJECT	INTERMINABLE
DESPONDENT	ELATION	FREE SPACE	PRODIGIOUS	VANQUISHED
SPECTER	FACETIOUS	DENOTED	OBDURATE	RELIANCE
MOROSE	IMPRECATIONS	CHAOS	REPROOF	OBLIGED

Red Badge of Courage Vocab

DAUNTLESS	IMPETUS	PERFUNCTORY	DISCONCERTED	MALEDICTION
ALTERCATION	AUDACIOUS	SULLEN	SINUOUS	VINDICATION
LUDICROUS	DENUNCIATION	FREE SPACE	PROXIMITY	IMPENDING
EXASPERATION	BEDRAGGLED	HEEDLESS	INDIGNANTLY	PONDEROUS
ANNIHILATED	PLACIDLY	DISCERNED	CONDESCENSION	OBLIGED

Red Badge of Courage Vocab

VANQUISHED	INDIGNANTLY	IMPETUS	SINUOUS	CHAOS
EXASPERATION	PROXIMITY	FORMIDABLE	ELATION	SARDONIC
PONDEROUS	OMINOUS	FREE SPACE	OBDURATE	CONDESCENSION
DELIRIUM	PERFUNCTORY	VINDICATION	IMPRECATIONS	AUDACIOUS
DISCERNED	ABJECT	HEEDLESS	REPOSE	ALTERCATION

Red Badge of Courage Vocab

ANNIHILATED	MOROSE	DAUNTLESS	FACETIOUS	OBSCURITY
IMPENDING	DENUNCIATION	SMITTEN	ORBS	DESPONDENT
DENOTED	OBLIGED	FREE SPACE	DISCONCERTED	INTERMINABLE
LUDICROUS	SULLEN	BLITHE	PLACIDLY	REPROOF
PRODIGIOUS	MALEDICTION	AGUE	SPECTER	ALTERCATION

Red Badge of Courage Vocab

RELIANCE	OBSCURITY	INDIGNANTLY	EXASPERATION	DENUNCIATION
REPOSE	SULLEN	MALEDICTION	DISCONCERTED	PLACIDLY
INTERMINABLE	DISCERNED	FREE SPACE	ANNIHILATED	IMPETUS
ALTERCATION	FACETIOUS	SINUOUS	ABJECT	BEDRAGGLED
SARDONIC	IMPRECATIONS	MOROSE	DESPONDENT	HEEDLESS

Red Badge of Courage Vocab

DELIRIUM	FORMIDABLE	VANQUISHED	PROXIMITY	SMITTEN
OBLIGED	CONDESCENSION	CHAOS	PERFUNCTORY	BLITHE
OBDURATE	SPECTER	FREE SPACE	LUDICROUS	DENOTED
VINDICATION	AUDACIOUS	PONDEROUS	ORBS	AGUE
ELATION	IMPENDING	DAUNTLESS	REPROOF	HEEDLESS

Red Badge of Courage Vocab

REPROOF	DENUNCIATION	EXASPERATION	FACETIOUS	MALEDICTION
PROXIMITY	AUDACIOUS	PLACIDLY	ANNIHILATED	PRODIGIOUS
AGUE	ALTERCATION	FREE SPACE	ELATION	SPECTER
ABJECT	BEDRAGGLED	SMITTEN	CHAOS	DAUNTLESS
INTERMINABLE	PERFUNCTORY	DESPONDENT	DISCERNED	MOROSE

Red Badge of Courage Vocab

REPOSE	LUDICROUS	SINUOUS	HEEDLESS	IMPETUS
DENOTED	INDIGNANTLY	OMINOUS	OBDURATE	VANQUISHED
SULLEN	IMPENDING	FREE SPACE	RELIANCE	SARDONIC
OBLIGED	IMPRECATIONS	ORBS	DELIRIUM	OBSCURITY
BLITHE	CONDESCENSION	VINDICATION	DISCONCERTED	MOROSE

Red Badge of Courage Vocab

IMPRECATIONS	DAUNTLESS	BLITHE	FORMIDABLE	DELIRIUM
DENUNCIATION	OBSCURITY	SARDONIC	REPROOF	DISCERNED
ANNIHILATED	SULLEN	FREE SPACE	AGUE	LUDICROUS
INDIGNANTLY	BEDRAGGLED	OMINOUS	DISCONCERTED	AUDACIOUS
RELIANCE	SINUOUS	PROXIMITY	IMPENDING	VANQUISHED

Red Badge of Courage Vocab

PLACIDLY	MALEDICTION	HEEDLESS	INTERMINABLE	IMPETUS
ABJECT	OBDURATE	PERFUNCTORY	CONDESCENSION	SMITTEN
OBLIGED	CHAOS	FREE SPACE	EXASPERATION	ELATION
DENOTED	FACETIOUS	ORBS	ALTERCATION	REPOSE
DESPONDENT	PRODIGIOUS	MOROSE	PONDEROUS	VANQUISHED

Red Badge of Courage Vocab

ORBS	SARDONIC	OBDURATE	CONDESCENSION	PLACIDLY
HEEDLESS	REPROOF	SMITTEN	DENUNCIATION	VANQUISHED
AGUE	MALEDICTION	FREE SPACE	DENOTED	REPOSE
DISCERNED	SINUOUS	PERFUNCTORY	BLITHE	IMPENDING
ANNIHILATED	SPECTER	PRODIGIOUS	BEDRAGGLED	OMINOUS

Red Badge of Courage Vocab

CHAOS	IMPRECATIONS	FACETIOUS	OBLIGED	DAUNTLESS
INTERMINABLE	ABJECT	ELATION	OBSCURITY	DISCONCERTED
VINDICATION	RELIANCE	FREE SPACE	ALTERCATION	LUDICROUS
PONDEROUS	INDIGNANTLY	MOROSE	FORMIDABLE	EXASPERATION
PROXIMITY	AUDACIOUS	DELIRIUM	DESPONDENT	OMINOUS

Red Badge of Courage Vocab

INDIGNANTLY	DENUNCIATION	CHAOS	ANNIHILATED	AGUE
IMPETUS	MOROSE	DELIRIUM	VANQUISHED	DENOTED
RELIANCE	BEDRAGGLED	FREE SPACE	REPOSE	DISCONCERTED
IMPENDING	FORMIDABLE	EXASPERATION	MALEDICTION	SINUOUS
PERFUNCTORY	ALTERCATION	DISCERNED	FACETIOUS	DAUNTLESS

Red Badge of Courage Vocab

HEEDLESS	SARDONIC	PLACIDLY	PONDEROUS	LUDICROUS
BLITHE	VINDICATION	SMITTEN	OMINOUS	SULLEN
ELATION	ORBS	FREE SPACE	SPECTER	PROXIMITY
PRODIGIOUS	OBLIGED	ABJECT	INTERMINABLE	OBDURATE
REPROOF	AUDACIOUS	CONDESCENSION	DESPONDENT	DAUNTLESS

Red Badge of Courage Vocab

IMPRECATIONS	PROXIMITY	DISCERNED	EXASPERATION	ABJECT
SINUOUS	AGUE	IMPENDING	ORBS	DISCONCERTED
ANNIHILATED	REPROOF	FREE SPACE	IMPETUS	ELATION
VANQUISHED	OBLIGED	SPECTER	CONDESCENSION	FORMIDABLE
MALEDICTION	PRODIGIOUS	PERFUNCTORY	OBDURATE	LUDICROUS

Red Badge of Courage Vocab

MOROSE	INDIGNANTLY	DENUNCIATION	INTERMINABLE	VINDICATION
SMITTEN	DESPONDENT	CHAOS	BLITHE	DAUNTLESS
BEDRAGGLED	AUDACIOUS	FREE SPACE	ALTERCATION	OMINOUS
SARDONIC	HEEDLESS	DELIRIUM	RELIANCE	OBSCURITY
FACETIOUS	REPOSE	SULLEN	PONDEROUS	LUDICROUS

www.ingramcontent.com/pod-product-compliance
Lightning Source LLC
Chambersburg PA
CBHW081456070526
44586CB00019B/2378